GIRL UP

GIRL UP

Laura Bates

**SIMON &
SCHUSTER**

London · New York · Sydney · Toronto · New Delhi

A CBS COMPANY

First published in Great Britain by Simon & Schuster UK Ltd, 2016
A CBS COMPANY

Copyright © 2016 by Laura Bates

3 5 7 9 10 8 6 4 2

Simon & Schuster UK Ltd
1st Floor
222 Gray's Inn Road
London WC1X 8HB

www.simonandschuster.co.uk

Simon & Schuster Australia, Sydney
Simon & Schuster India, New Delhi

Illustrations copyright © 2016 by Jo Harrison

A CIP catalogue record for this book
is available from the British Library.

ISBN: 978-1-4711-4950-4
Ebook ISBN: 978-1-4711-4951-1

Typeset in Meta by M Rules
Printed in Italy by L.E.G.O SpA

CONTENTS

Buckle UP   xi

1. Fakebook, Fitter and Instaglam   1
2. You Aren't Your Body   24
3. Making Waves   56
4. 'Mean Girls' and Mental Health   77
5. That's Not Your Vagina   98
6. Don't Be Shy, Aim High   133
7. Sluts, Unicorns and Other Mythical Creatures   160
8. It's My Face and I'll Smile if I Want to   191
9. Clitorish Allsorts   217
10. Circle of Shame   249
11. Porn ≠ Sex   275
12. The F-Word   292

Girl UP   313

Acknowledgements   315

Resources and Further Information   317

Notes   323

BUCKLE UP

You've been getting messages since you were a baby. Messages about who you are and what you're good at, about how the world sees you and what you should do if you want to succeed.

They're the kind of messages you don't really think about because they are all around you, all the time.

They said you need to be thin and beautiful.

They told you to wear longer skirts, avoid going out late at night and move in groups. Never accept drinks from a stranger, and wear shoes you can run in more easily than heels.

They instructed you to wear just enough make-up to look 'presentable' but not enough to be a slag; to dress to flatter your apple, pear, hourglass figure, but not to be too slutty.

They warned you if you're strong, opinionated, or take control, you'll be shrill, bossy, a ballbreaker.

They asked you why you can't take a joke.

They informed you that you should know your place.

They told you 'that's not for girls'; 'take it as a compliment'; 'don't rock the boat'; 'that'll go straight to your hips'; 'smile darling. They told you that 'beauty is on the inside' but you knew they didn't really mean it.

Well, fuck that. I'm here to tell you something else.

*　*　*

I want to give you a heads-up at the beginning that this book is quite rude. It contains dancing vaginas, discussions about sex and colour-by-numbers genitalia.

Things this book is not:

- Abstinent
- Self-hating
- Pink
- Polite

Things for which this book has zero fucks to give:

- Societal expectations
- Societal judgement
- Gender stereotypes
- Any form of prejudice
- Sexist jokes
- Cronuts (why would you take a perfectly good doughnut and make it all dry and flaky? Just why?)

In this book, I will sometimes talk about 'people with vaginas', or 'people who are attracted to men', or 'self-defining women'. This might seem weird and unnecessary. You may think all these could be covered by using the word 'woman'.

It's understandable that you might think that, because we live in a world that likes things to be black and white. We live in a world that likes us to stay inside the lines, in nice, simple boxes. But people don't always fit into boxes. Some people are attracted to others of the same sex. Some people are attracted to people of various different sexes. Some people aren't attracted to anyone at all. Some people know (often from a very young age) that they don't match the gender that was assigned to them at birth. Some people feel like they fall on a spectrum of gender outside the societal categories of 'male' or 'female'. All this means that we can't just assume everybody with a vagina is a woman, say, or that all women have vaginas. It means we can't assume that all women are only attracted to men and vice versa. It means 'women' and 'men' aren't the only two types of people.

It's pretty simple, and it's not a big deal to include everybody in our picture of the world, even if it means the picture isn't quite as boxy and orderly as before. Sometimes I'll use the acronym LGBT* to refer to people with different sexual orientations and gender identities. This includes lesbian, gay, bisexual and transgender, but the asterisk is there to indicate that there are lots of other categories included too, like agender, asexual, queer, intersex, gender fluid etc.

Some people think this stuff is tedious and annoying, especially if it requires an explanation like this at the beginning of a book. But just think, if everybody got the hell on board with this message, it would quickly become so normal that we wouldn't have to spell it out any more. Let's say maybe all the books written between 2016 and 2018 mentioned it, and then it'd be so widely known that we'd be done with the explanations. It would have a big positive impact for folk who are currently often left out of the picture altogether, without hurting others in the slightest.

And let's face it, if you've already decided to read the other 71,235 words of this book, how far are an extra hundred here or there really putting you out?

Wait, don't be put off by the whole 71,235-word thing ... There are pictures ... COME BACK!

Just to warn you about what you're getting yourself into before you go any further, here is a list of alternative titles that were considered for this book:

Spunk for Girls
Whose Vagina Is It Anyway?
Tinker Tailor Soldier Slut
Bend Clit like Beckham
Men Are from Earth, Women Are from Earth
Revulva
The Dangerous Book for Girls
The Fanny Pack

–

You have been warned.

I'm writing this book because I've spent a lot of time travelling up and down the country and around the world meeting girls and young women and talking to them about their experiences. I run a website called the Everyday Sexism Project, where people of all ages can share their experiences of any kind of sexism, harassment, discrimination or assault. One of the things that completely knocked me off my feet was the number of young people who were writing in, sharing what they were putting up with. And wow, were young women dealing with a lot of crap.

Mostly they were twisting themselves into pretzel-shaped knots trying to cope with the world giving them approximately 452 gazillion instructions on how to be the *perfect* girl, to turn into the *perfect* woman, to have the *perfect* skin and the *perfect* grades and the *perfect* relationship and the *perfect* body and the *perfect* sex and the *perfect* career and the *perfect* bikini for their body shape and it all just seemed *perfectly* exhausting. But while the world is in the middle of giving them all these absurdly specific instructions, it also really likes to bash them at the same time. Because that seems fair. All things considered, girls and young women get a ridiculously bad rep.

'What are you, a girl?'

'You throw like a girl.'

'You run like a girl.'

'My little sister could do better than you.'

'Why are you being such a girl?'

Um, hello? Most young women are the only people on the planet who are simultaneously coping with a turbo cocktail of hormones; the challenge presented by growing unwieldy new body parts; a sudden propensity to bleed all over the place once a month, which can hurt like hell; overwhelming academic pressure; and, on top of it all, your crappy global stereotypes about GIRLS BEING GENERALLY RUBBISH AT EVERYTHING!

Oh, and no big deal or anything, but *today's* young women also just happen to be the first generation since the dinosaurs to be going through all this under the all-seeing, all-commenting, all-tweeting eye that is 360 degree, 24/7 social media. #YouveGotToBeKiddingMe

Do you see David Cameron coping with any of that shit? (Though to be fair, he *does* struggle with Twitter sometimes.)

Young women are superheroes.

If people actually realized how much teenage girls are up against, there'd be a hell of a lot more respect for them. And maybe some pretty spectacular parades. And medals. Lots of medals.

If we could just harness the international power of teenage girls we could probably topple at least twelve dictatorships, reverse global warming and pretty much sort out world peace by lunchtime. I'm actually not even kidding. Young women face sexism, stereotyping, media objectification and huge double standards. If we could just crack all that then we'd be tapping into the most enormous surge of brain power the world has to offer – and within a few years those same young women could go on to jobs where they'd really get shit done. This idea has legs, NASA, and you can have it for free. (I don't know, I just kind of feel like dealing with massive world problems is mostly NASA's responsibility.) You're welcome, guys.

Which brings me on to another point. See how I just used the word 'guys' to mean 'a group of people'?

This is one of those tiny-little-nagging, 'normal' things that happen all around us without us ever really noticing. But they whisper. They're doing it right now. Can you hear it? *Psssssst. Girls aren't that big of a deal. Guys are what really matter. Let's just assume that when we talk about people we really mean men. Let's label all the big jobs with 'man' on the end to remind girls that the import- ant stuff gets done by policemen and firemen and businessmen.*

Or take the phrase 'man up'. It's used to mean 'get on with it'; 'be courageous'; 'grab the bull by the horns'. It suggests that men who are timid, or hesitant, or upset are somehow failing at being manly enough. *And* it tells girls that strength and courage and decisive- ness are male qualities. But why should they be? Why shouldn't 'girl up' mean; 'be strong'; 'go for it'; 'do it your own way'? Why can't strength include being emotional too? Regardless of sex! Girls are some of the bravest, strongest people in the world, after all.

This book isn't taking any of that crap lying down. This book will call it how it sees it. This book has its own sexist bullshit klaxon. This book is the iron-clad, no nonsense, elastic reinforced, slap-em-on and get shit done, white pants of books. (If books were underwear.) This book is the heroic, indomitable, slick it back, tie it up, don't bother curling, who needs conditioner, any old elastic band will do, ponytail of books. (If books were hairstyles.) This book is the get down to business, stick it on and forget about it, ultra-absorbent, triple length, extra wings, night time use, heavy flow, who cares about the plasticky sound, sanitary towel of books. (If books were sanitary protection.)

[Editor's note: This book is getting off course.]

Right. Let's get started.

CHAPTER ONE

FAKEBOOK, FITTER AND INSTAGLAM

Before social media, the internet was a bit like an electronic version of a library. It provided a lot of information at your fingertips, a wealth of documents on obscure topics, old news reports and some sneaky snuggling in the back. Since social media arrived, internet users have stepped inside the screen and become part of its content. Suddenly our lives, our looks, our relationships, our meals and our cats are open to scrutiny. Suddenly we all know when a guy we were at primary school with is contemplating whether to have a biscuit or not. Suddenly we have become the material other people are poring over. The internet has become less like a library and more like a computer game, where you steer your character through different challenges and compete to earn social points and level up. But the game is very different for girls than it is for guys ...

STEP 1: Select your avatar

For guys: This can be pretty much any nice picture of you.

+10 bonus points for getting started so quickly.

For girls: Think carefully. This picture will have a serious impact on your success as you proceed through the game. What?! NOT THAT ONE! Are you serious?

+3 points if you reveal some flesh

+5 points if you reveal cleavage or legs

−5 points if the cleavage is too low and considered slutty

−10 points if you reveal both legs and cleavage

+6 points for an arty Instagram filter

−8 points if your picture looks too filtered and fake

You just lost 5 hours' sleep and skipped 3 homework assignments: LOSE A LIFE

STEP 2: Set up a social media account

For guys: +5 bonus points for quickly attracting 100 followers: LEVEL UP

For girls: −5 points for failing to attract as many followers as your male peers

10 minutes after setting up your account you receive your first unsolicited dick pic: LOSE A LIFE

STEP 3: Create your first post – a comment on a recent news story

For guys: Your post is 'liked' or reblogged/retweeted/shared 15 times +10 points

For girls: Someone writes a sarcastic sexist comment on your post −5 points

Someone questions whether you actually know anything about the topic −7 points

STEP 4: Post an artistic picture that happens to show the merest edge of your nipple

For guys: Your post is liked a few times +5 points

For girls: Your account is suspended for 2 weeks −10 points

STEP 5: Post a strong opinion about something

For guys: Several people like and agree with your post +5 points

A few people disagree and post their own points of view −2 points

For girls: Receive 3 rape threats −40 points

If you are LGBT*/disabled/non-white the abuse is worse and mixed with racism/transphobia/ableism/homophobia −40 points

Your post is shared on 4Chan and people start making violent and abusive comments: LOSE A LIFE

Someone finds and posts your home address online −40 points

You report the threats and abuse but the automatic response says they don't violate community rules −15 points

You are so shocked about the abuse that you screenshot it and post it from your own account to show people how bad it is. Your account is suspended for violating community rules.

GAME OVER

This might sound a bit exaggerated, and of course it's true that guys can have a hard time online too, but generally speaking this is a pretty realistic picture of the difference between using the internet while presenting as male vs presenting as female.

Studies have found that users are more likely to follow men than women on Twitter,[1] and men are around twice as likely to be retweeted as women.[2] In lists of the most influential social media users, men almost always dominate. When Australian feminist writer Clementine Ford received a torrent of abusive and misogynistic messages from men on Facebook, she reposted some of them to show how bad the problem was, including screenshots of Facebook saying they didn't violate community guidelines. But Ford's own account was suspended for violating the rules.

UK Children's Laureate Malorie Blackman received a wave of racist and sexist abuse on Twitter just for saying that children's books ought to have a diverse range of characters. How dare she?

Caroline Criado-Perez received hundreds of rape and death threats because she had the audacity to suggest that it might be nice to have just one woman among the notable people featured on our bank notes. What an outrageous and disgusting suggestion!

Several people have written about experiments they've done where they set up two Twitter accounts, one in a woman's name and one in a man's. When they tweeted the same opinions on political issues from both accounts, the 'men' were listened to, engaged with, and retweeted, but the 'women' were questioned, ridiculed, and abused.[3]

All this makes it sound like the online world isn't much fun for women and girls. But it can also be an amazing source of support, friendship and information. And pressure is on social media companies to tackle the problem. In the meantime, it's just sensible to be aware of the potential downsides, though hopefully you won't experience them yourself. And the good news is that there's lots you can do to protect yourself and stay safe online.

The easiest way to protect yourself online is to think of the online space as if it were a real space – think of your social media accounts like your home.

If you wouldn't invite strangers into your home, don't let people you don't know access your profiles or accept their friend requests.

If you wouldn't let a stranger in the street start flicking through the pics on your phone, don't share images with someone you don't know online.

You also don't have to go online if you don't feel like it – it's OK to take breaks from social media. In fact, it's distinctly advisable. If you spend too much time glued to the screen you start to go weirdly electronic and forget how to communicate effectively with real humans (which is a vital skill, especially if you plan to have all the sex). Like when you get too dependent on WhatsApp and when you talk to people face-to-face, instead of using your words you just start going:

or

and you end up being all like:

Where were we? Right, treating the online world like the real one.

If you wouldn't put up with someone shouting abuse at you outside your house then shut the door on them when they do it online too – block their account.

If a real-life stranger started contacting and following you you'd probably tell a trusted friend or someone who could help – you can do the same if it happens online.

If someone makes you feel unsafe by hanging around, following you from one place to another or harassing you, you can report them to the social media company as well as raising the alarm in real life. If they threaten to hurt or rape you, or seem to be stalking you, you can also report them to the police. These things are just as illegal online as they are in real life.

The way you respond to online harassment is 100 per cent up to you. If it feels powerful to respond or retweet, that's okay. If you prefer to log off and take a break, that's fine too.

TOP 10 TIPS FOR STAYING SAFE ONLINE

1. Privacy Settings

All social media accounts come with privacy settings – have a look at them and make sure they are set so that strangers can't access and view your information. This doesn't mean your friends won't be able to find you, but it means you are in control of who sees your stuff.

2. Pictures

You can usually set individual privacy settings for pictures too. Remember, a picture online is a bit like a race horse – once it gets out of the gate there's no stopping it and also it's going to eat you out of house and home with all the oats and hay and stuff it needs. (No, wait, that's just race horses.) Seriously though, even if you delete a picture it could already have been copied and shared by someone else, so the only way to completely control what pictures are out there is to think carefully about what you put up in the first place and what privacy settings you put against it.

3. Passwords

A 'strong' password is one nobody else could guess – so don't use family or pet names, dates of birth etc. Adding numbers and symbols also increases strength, so for example: H£yScumb@gStopH@ck1ngMyaccountYouLos3r would be a super strong password. And keep your passwords separate so you have a different one for each online account – that way even if someone hacked into your email or Facebook they wouldn't be able to access your online banking or your Tumblr.

4. Personal Information

Never put your address, phone number, what school/uni/ college you go to or any other personal details online. Don't give them out to anyone who contacts you online either. 'Why could you possibly need to know?' is a solid question to ask here.

5. Two-Step Verification

This is a nifty setting available on most email and social media accounts. It's a bit of a faff but (like sanitary towels with wings) it's worth it if you want to stay extra secure. You add a phone number to your account and when you access your profile from a new computer you get a code texted to you to verify it's you and not someone else trying to get in. Also great for boosting your popularity with all those extra text messages ;)

6. Reporting

Social media companies are running a business just like anyone else and they have a responsibility to keep their users safe. If someone is harassing you online or sending abusive messages, take a screenshot, block their profile and use whatever reporting function is available.

7. Stranger Danger

Remember anyone can set up a social media profile using photos they've stolen from elsewhere online and all is not always what it seems. This DOES mean: being wary of people you don't know who befriend you online – remember, they may not be who they say they are. This DOESN'T mean: challenging that kid from next door about whether he Photoshopped those pictures where he claims to have met Dr Who. Bless him; he's got enough problems already.

8. Keep it Online

Don't agree to meet someone offline unless a) you already know them IRL or b) it's Harry Styles. I'M KIDDING, THAT WAS A TEST! DON'T *EVER* MEET SOMEONE OFFLINE WHO CLAIMS TO BE HARRY STYLES ON THE INTERNET.

9. Think Before You Post

This sounds obvious, but the internet has done this weird thing where it's taken away the feeling that we're talking to a real person and the time we had in the good old days to think before communicating with them. I bet nobody in Victorian times had to rush over in a horse and cart to take back the snarky comment they'd telegrammed about a friend's latest portrait. As a general rule, if you wouldn't say it to someone's face IRL you probably shouldn't say it online. In fact, saying something out loud before you post it is a brilliant way to see whether it sounds completely ridiculous before you click that button and it's too late to take it back.

10. Help Is Available

You're never alone. If anything goes wrong or feels scary online, it's probably best to talk to someone about it, just to set your mind at rest. Talk to a friend or someone you trust, and if you don't feel able to talk to someone you know, there are great organizations like the Cybersmile Foundation (details in the back of the book), which can provide support over email, phone, Twitter, Tumblr or Facebook. (And wow, do they have one exhausted social media staffer.)

All this is fairly easily done, and the occasional downsides shouldn't put you off using social media if you want to. In fact, here are some incredible things that young people have done using social media:

- When twenty-one-year-old Katie Cutler heard a story about a local disabled pensioner who had been attacked and thrown to the ground outside his own home, breaking his collarbone, she couldn't stop thinking about it. She set up a funding campaign to raise money to support Alan Barnes, using social media to raise awareness about the story and hoping to attract £500 in donations to help him get back on his feet. Instead, the story went viral and she raised over £300,000 – enough to help Mr Barnes move to a new home. She went on to found the Katie Cutler Foundation, raising funds to help others in need.

- In October 2012, a group of amazing teenage girls decided they wanted to find out more about feminism, and create a safe space for others to discuss, learn and talk about feminism too. So they started the Twitter Youth Feminist Army, which quickly swelled to an international movement spreading the word about feminism, campaigning on issues like consent and encouraging people to join the movement.

- American teenager Lena Strickling, eighteen, has a form of cancer called Hodgkin's lymphoma. She was contacted by the Make-A-Wish Foundation, who probably expected her to use her wish to go skydiving or meet a celebrity like most people. But Lena wasn't most people. She used her wish to make a viral video sharing her story of being sexually abused by her father from a young age – to help spread awareness, tackle stigma and inspire other victims to feel they could reach out for support.

Alongside the bad and the good of the online world comes the downright weird. How on earth did we get to the point where it was semi-normal to send someone a picture of your semi-erect penis? WHAT THE HELL, GUYS! (In this case I don't think we need a sexist bullshit klaxon because I am literally referring mostly to the guys. Sort it out, chaps.)

How do we live in a world where we might be confronted, at any moment, with the delightful surprise that is a little, naked cock jauntily popping up in our inbox? How do we respond, when confronted with these pioneers of twenty-first-century chivalry?

Well, you have options. I'm not going to tell you to turn off your computer or shut down your social media profiles because that's about as useful as telling someone whose keyboard isn't working to press 'ctrl alt delete'. We need to be able to function in online spaces and being pushed out of them by online misogyny isn't a great solution for young women. If you feel happier deleting unsolicited dick pics or just turning the computer off, that's absolutely fine – whatever feels best for you is definitely the way to go. But if you'd prefer to push back, here are a few ideas . . .

Reply with a legion of sad faces (no one wants this response to a snazzy snapshot of their todger):

☹☹☹☹☹☹☹☹☹☹☹☹☹☹☹☹☹☹☹☹☹☹☹☹☹☹☹☹☹☹
☹☹☹☹☹☹☹☹☹☹☹☹☹☹☹☹☹☹☹☹☹☹☹☹☹☹☹☹☹☹
☹☹☹☹☹☹☹☹☹☹☹☹☹☹☹☹☹☹☹☹☹☹☹☹☹☹☹☹☹☹
☹☹☹☹☹☹☹☹☹☹☹☹☹☹☹☹☹☹☹☹☹☹☹☹☹☹☹☹☹☹
☹☹☹☹☹☹☹☹☹☹☹☹☹☹☹☹☹☹☹☹☹☹☹☹☹☹☹☹☹☹

Keep it short and sweet:

'Haha! NO.'

Play 'em at their own game:

If you are unlucky enough to be the proud recipient of more than one unwelcome dick pic, try the following method: keep the first one in a file somewhere and when you receive the next one, send them back the picture of the other guy's penis.

Hey, he clearly thinks it's a real treat to be sent one, right? How could he be anything but thrilled?

(Note: this only applies if you and your persuasive Romeo are over eighteen – see below.)

Alternatively, on the next page there are a few pre-prepared responses for unsolicited dick pics that are handily sized for snapping with your smart phone and pinging right back into their inbox.

Of course, it's not just dealing with other people's unwanted body parts that gets tricky online or on your phone. It's often what people want you to do with yours too.

When you're a young woman, you're basically stuck between a rock and a hard place. This expression comes from the Greek legend of Scylla and Charybdis, mythical sea monsters which feature in Homer's *The Odyssey*. Basically Charybdis is a massive scary whirlpool that sucks your ship in and kills everybody on board and Scylla is a six-headed beast that munches your sailors up without so much as a 'would you mind if I ate you now, please?' Unfortunately they're very close together, so you essentially have no choice but to sail close to one or the other. Why nobody ever just sails around the long way is not discussed.

In the book, Odysseus chooses to swing by Scylla and risk losing a few sailors rather than go closer to Charybdis and risk losing the whole ship. (Bet the few sailors who got munched didn't find this a particularly noble choice.) Anyway, if Homer had

lived in the twenty-first century, the story would basically have featured a female heroine called Odyssea (because Homer is hip and would totally have got with the times), who has to choose between sending a nude pic, risking the slut-shaming whirlpool of the whole school calling her a whore, or refusing and being called an uptight prude by her Cyclops boyfriend. (I'm slightly changing the storyline, OK.) It feels like you can't win. So what do you do?

Again, a lot of this is about knowing your own gut and working out what feels right to you. I'm not saying you should never share pictures with someone you're intimate with and completely trust. It's your body after all. But if you don't feel 100 per cent comfortable then you should never be pushed into 'sexting', or sending pics of yourself that you don't want to. And even if you do feel 100 per cent comfortable there are still a few things to think about first . . .

Important things to know:

- If you are under eighteen, 'sexting' is 100 per cent illegal. Yup, even though the age of consent is sixteen, taking, sharing or uploading any erotic pic of someone under eighteen is a crime – it is classed as an 'indecent image of a child'.

- This includes pictures of yourself – so even if you were sharing a pic of your own bits, it'd still be illegal if you are under eighteen.

- Taking, sharing or spreading nude pics of anyone else is not cool. Imagine how you'd feel if it happened to you.

- There isn't really a 'safe' way to share nude pics – as soon as it leaves your inbox it's out there and there's not much you can do to get it back. Even on Snapchat someone can still screengrab a pic and then it's out of your hands.

- Beware false promises. I've met so many girls whose boyfriends promised to keep naked pics private but then shared them with their friends. Real charmers. If you have even the tiniest nagging worry a picture might go further than you'd like, then the person you're sending it to probably doesn't deserve it.

But the trouble is, it's a lot easier to write down all the problems with sharing nude pics than it is to actually say no if someone asks you. A boyfriend/girlfriend might ask for it as a way of showing you love or trust them. Someone might say you're frigid or uptight if you refuse. They might say they won't be with you any more if you don't do it. You might feel like everybody else is doing it.

So how do you say no?

First of all, it's worth remembering that a partner who says they'll only want you or stay with you if you do something is a bully. Simple as that. It's not a relationship if you're pressured into doing something you're uncomfortable with.

And even if everyone else says they're doing it, it doesn't necessarily mean that they are. The people who brag the most about things are almost always the ones who have a lot of talking time because they're not actually doing anything.

Like with dick pics, it can be a lot easier to respond to requests for nudes with something silly or funny than to feel like you have to just say no.

So here are a few possible responses:

If he asks to see your tits...
send him a pair (with one giving
the middle feather, just for
good measure)...

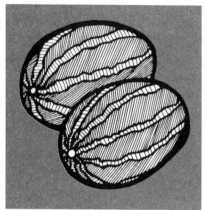

Or perhaps send him some
lovely melons...

Or a pair of jugs...

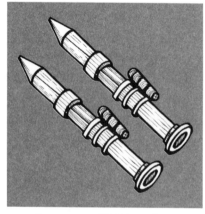

Or even some HUGE bazookas...

For a more low-tech response, if someone asks you to send a nude, you can always send this:

NUDE.

Hope you enjoy.

And this helpful reply is useful for a wide variety of occasions, including dick pics and nude demands:

Thank you for your application for the position of : *'lover'*.

Unfortunately your application was not successful.

You may wish to work on your awareness of: tone, content and audience.

We wish you every luck in your future endeavours.

Sometimes, if you have sent a nude pic (or even if you haven't), things can get out of hand fast. One young woman who shared her story on the Everyday Sexism website wrote: 'Yesterday at school I was sat at a desk working, and didn't notice a male friend of mine take a picture of my breasts. The only reason I found out is because he Snapchatted the picture to various other guys from my school, having edited it so that my breasts were circled.'

If something like this happens, or if someone shares a picture you sent them without your permission, they may well be breaking the law (both the actual law of the land and the social law against being a total arse-trumpeting shitweasel). This isn't an easy thing to deal with, but you have options. You can contact an anti-bullying helpline for support (details in the back of the book). You can talk to somebody you trust about it, or report it to your school, college or university, though you may understandably not feel able to take this step. Most importantly remember that the person who deserves to be thoroughly ashamed of themselves is not you for one moment, but the asswipe spreading your picture around without your permission. One of the most powerful things we can do in situations like this is to support the person it is happening to. If every time something like this happened, everyone else in the school rallied around the victim and called out the guys sharing the picture, it would have much less severe consequences. And the person who spread the picture without permission would think twice about doing it again.

Sadly, growing up in the twenty-first century also means dealing with the twenty-first-century chat-up line. Gone are the days of a nice stroll together in the park, a casual chat at a friend's party or a dance in a club. Gone are the joys of the subtle approach, the flirtatious small talk, the nudges and smiles. We are living in the glorious new age of 'Hey nice pic, FANCY A FUCK?'

Everything from text messages to WhatsApp, Tinder to Snapchat has readied our inboxes for the onslaught of over-sexed, over-confident, ovary-shrivelling pick-up lines. The aggression. The terrible spelling. If that's your thing, cool. If not, what do you do?

Well, fear not. You're lucky enough to be hearing from someone who once genuinely experienced the darling pick-up line: 'Did you just fart? Because you blew me away.'

So trust me when I say these responses will work. I am sorry to have to inform you that the following are all real examples, gathered through painful experience by my long-suffering girlfriends and crowdsourced from other women online.

They say: Nice dress. Can I talk you out of it?
You say: Nice trousers. Can I pay you to keep them on?

They say: Are you a cowgirl? Cos I can see you riding me.
You say: Are you the back end of a pantomime horse? Cos you should quit while you're behind.

They say: Are you spring? Cos you'll be coming soon.
You say: Are you winter? Cos you're leaving me cold.

They say: Are you a termite? Because you're about to get a mouthful of wood.
You say: Are you a wild pig? Because you boar me to tears.

They say: Are your legs made of butter? Because I'd love to spread them.
You say: Are your pick-up lines made of Marmite? Because they totally stink.

They say: **My dick's not going to suck itself.**
You say: **It's obviously got great taste.**

* * *

Now, don't get me started on the sites, memes and content that put young women down. You've seen it. We all have. The meme about drugging girls, or hitting or raping them. The 'jokes' and 'lad banter'. The Cleavage Thursdays and the 'Spotted' pages and the ratings out of ten. That stupid thing where they circle all the 'flaws' on a beautiful girl and label her '2/10 would not bang'. The pages about wenches and hoes and skanks and clunge and gash and chicks and tramps and sloppy seconds. The memes about locks and keys and vaginas and blondes and tits and bangability. Anonymous Q & A websites where the questions are violent and graphic. Nasty comments about your appearance or your pictures.

Feel sorry for them. These guys are spending so much time jizzing their frustration, rage and misogyny over the keyboard that they've never even met a real-life girl. The nastiness and the comments come from a place of insecurity and panic – the internet lets you spew out all your own worries on someone else.

This is another time to think about the internet as if it were a real place. If someone is being hateful, report them. If you see someone being nasty to a friend or somebody you know, stick up for them. Neutralise a mean comment by adding a nice one. If someone is getting hurtful tweets or comments, message them and check they're OK. Stand up for each other.

This goes for nasty messages and comments from girls too. When we occupy an online world that sets us up against one another, competing for the most likes and retweets can make us all feel panicked. Like we're all scrambling for currency but there isn't quite enough to go around. It sometimes feels like one way to get a bit more security for yourself is to join in with putting other people down and laughing at other girls to make sure it's not you being criticized. It's normal and understandable that this happens – girls can bully one another online as much as guys can. But we also have the choice to stand up to it together. If guys are treating one girl in a sexist way online, joining in doesn't make you immune, it means you're adding to a problem that could later affect you too.

On the upside, when you see nasty behaviour online, just think, the internet is actually providing a much-needed public service – it weeds out the dickheads so you don't have to. What's sexier than a guy sharing a rapey online meme? Pretty much anything else in the universe. If you see a guy liking or sharing a sexist meme you can swiftly add a 'stay away from this loser' flashing sign to him in your mind. Or, to put it in terms he might understand:

JACKASSES:
0/10

WOULD NOT BANG

CHAPTER TWO

YOU AREN'T YOUR BODY

Worrying about our bodies is a trap. It's a great big, ugly trick that keeps girls quiet and under-confident. It is used to keep them occupied and small and it stops them from being and doing whatever they want to be and do. (Unless what they want to be and do is hungry and laughing alone with salad.) It has been used against women for centuries and we are only just now wising up to it. But wising up to it doesn't always make it any easier to tackle.

Entirely unscientific data klaxon: let's say in one day you see 6 x TV adverts and pass 5 x billboards. Along the sides of the bus you take into town there are 12 x adverts. On the way, you quickly check your email, seeing 10 x pop-up ads as you click in and out of your inbox. When you go into Boots to get a Meal Deal for lunch there are pictures of women in bikinis on 4 x sandwiches and salads. To go to the till you walk past a cardboard cut-out of a very thin woman in a swimsuit advertising suncream. You take your lunch to the park, walking past 25 x size 6–8 mannequins in shop windows and another 20 x billboards. You then pass 15 x lingerie adverts as you go down the escalator into the tube. As you wait for the tube to pull in an enormous yellow poster screams, 'Are you beach body ready?' (Why, thank you so much, kind poster, for asking – that was *exactly* what I wanted to think about on my tired commute home.) You get the idea.

By the time you go to bed that night you've seen approximately 100 x women's bodies. If you took a random sample of 100 women from the population and looked at their bodies, it would look something like this ...

ALL BODIES ARE GOOD BODIES

A MERE SELECTION OF THE **VAST** ARRAY OF WONDERFUL WOMEN'S BODIES

According to the Office for National Statistics, the average woman in England is 5 foot 3 inches tall and weighs 11 stone. Her dress size is 16. (She also has 1.96 children, which sounds painful for everybody involved.)[1] But the women you see plastered across billboards and buses and magazines each day as you go about your life aren't average women. Far from it. You might have seen 100 women in one day, but you've really only seen one woman – you've just seen her picture 100 times. She is almost always tall, young, thin, white, conventionally beautiful, made-up, long-legged and large-breasted.

And as if using only the same type of body over and over wasn't enough, they go and chop bits and pieces off willy-nilly, using Photoshop so that *even* a tall-young-thin-white-beautiful-made-up-long-legged-large-breasted supermodel could pop down the shops and come home feeling crap about herself! Because the pictures are doctored! The game is rigged! IT'S A SET-UP, I TELL YOU, A SET-UP!

Ahem.

Now, because you've seen 100 pictures of her, it's easy to think she represents women more widely. After all, she's everywhere. (And WOW, do those numbers add up ... by the age of twelve, the average American teenage girl has seen up to 77,546 adverts!)[2] When you see her you automatically think about the jiggle in your own tummy, or how your thighs don't look like that, or how much sexier her wrists are than yours. (Don't tell me you haven't seen those sexy watch adverts.) You start to wish you had a thigh gap. (It seems to me that the easiest way to get a thigh gap is to sit cross-legged, but what do I know? Am I doing this right?)

You might start to feel pretty rubbish about yourself.

Let's say you only notice a quarter of these 100 pictures, and that you spend two minutes thinking about your body each time. That's nearly a whole hour of each day wasted thinking and worrying about the way we look. Seven hours a week. Thirty hours a month. 360 hours a year. That's over two weeks every year.

Just think of what you could do with those two weeks per year if you were no longer worrying about the size of your thighs! You could try outdoor swimming, memorize a tube map, become excellent at handstands or even take up curling.

A common panic when we see pictures of women on billboards or buses is to worry that potential partners are seeing them too and will expect us to look that way, or be disappointed when we don't. But remember these three important facts:

1. Any potential partner will know lots of women and girls, including their mums, sisters, cousins etc. So they're aware that 'real' women don't necessarily look the way women on posters do. And if they're worth your time they won't be judging you on your looks anyway.

2. If it's guys you're into, remember that they are also bombarded with idealized images of men, so they're familiar with the pressure and can probably relate. They're also likely to be so busy worrying about their own looks that they're pretty grateful for any attention from you, not waiting with a magazine and a tape measure to see how you measure up.

3. Most people are much less observant about other people's looks than they are about their own. You could probably walk around with COCK written on your forehead in marker pen and only about 50 per cent of people would even notice. (Don't try this.) We are not particularly aware of small changes in other people's bodies, we tend just to worry about our own.

Still, it is very easy to feel that, as a girl, you should be dieting, and thinking about losing weight, pretty much constantly. When I go into schools and talk to girls, 'looks', 'weight' and 'size' are some of the most common things they say they worry about. It's understandable – when famous women are interviewed, they are very often asked how they stay slim, and everywhere we look we see miracle diets, eating plans and detox cleanses being advertised in a pushy, shouty way.

It's funny, because not so long ago curviness and bigger bodies were actually considered the 'ideal' form for women (just look at some of the nude paintings and voluptuous statues you see in art galleries). It's only relatively recently that being as thin as possible has become the holy grail of womanly 'perfection'. In fact, if you look back over the years, women's 'ideal' body shape fluctuates a lot, showing once and for all that the whole idea is nonsense and completely made-up!

People who are invested in this state of affairs (where women are so preoccupied with worrying about their weight that few of us are able to fully master curling) try to keep it going by making out that there's *nothing* more spectacularly fun and fabulous for girls than dieting and losing weight. (It's a profitable status quo for those in the media, fashion and diet industries among many others.) That's why there are such a terrifying number of stock photographs of women laughing alone with salads. It's also why you may have heard it said that 'nothing tastes better than skinny feels'.

You would not catch anyone trying to sell this kind of bullshit to men. Hey, guys! Nothing is more fun than cleaning the bathroom floor! Honestly! Try it! You'll never play a video game again! What's that? Get in the sea? OK then.

For the record, here is a list of things that taste better than skinny feels:

Lasagne

Pizza

Sushi   Paninis

Ice cream   Fajitas

Yoghurt

Curry

Doughnuts   Naan bread

Sausages

Almonds

Noodles

Fresh fruit

Spring rolls

Burritos

Spaghetti   Prawn crackers

Omelettes

Burgers

Cheese   Custard

Beans on toast

Chips   Chocolate

Cookies

Toast

Milkshakes

Roast chicken   Rice pudding

Porridge

Fish

Soup

Roast potatoes

Spam

Baked potatoes

Crusts

Tuna

Any kind of potatoes

Fresh bread

Sweetcorn

Blueberries

Tomatoes

Danish pastries

Trifle

Marshmallows

Hot chocolate

Pancakes

Chocolate cornflake cakes

Profiteroles

Croissants

Flatbread

Granola bars

Hoisin duck

Roast beef

Sorbet

Pork chops

Cucumber sandwiches

Baked Camembert

Popsicles

Cake pops

Popcorn

Jalapeño peppers

Lollipops

Pop Tarts

Popcorn chicken

Popping candy

Popcorn shrimp

Coco Pops

Lemon and poppy seed muffins

Here's a list of things that do not taste as good as skinny feels:

Pistachio ice cream

I'm being flippant, of course. And I don't mean for one second to undermine the very real and compelling severity of eating disorders. But I do mean to attack and ridicule the idea that as women and girls our value is in our thinness. And I do mean to bring as low as I possibly can the idea that being thin is more important than our own pleasure and enjoyment in life, whether that is in the form of eating or anything else.

To begin with, the things that start the earliest are often the hardest to shake off. The idea of our body as a disappointing problem that never matches up to our hopes starts very early indeed. In fact, research shows it starts at the age of five.[3] Before we even know the words to articulate the idea of body image pressure, we girls learn to worry about our shape. By the time we are seven years old, 25 per cent of us have tried to lose weight.[4] By the time we reach the age of ten, that number is estimated to rise to 80 per cent.[5] When so many of us are worrying and obsessing over our size, it becomes accepted as normal and even considered a 'girly' thing to do.

We might trick ourselves into thinking it's not really a 'diet', because we're not following a set of instructions, or only eating celery. But perhaps we stop ourselves from having any sweets, or make our portions smaller and smaller, or start skipping meals. Perhaps we make ourselves feel bad or 'punish' ourselves if we don't manage to keep to the rules we've created in our heads.

But it isn't normal. It isn't just 'part of being a girl', or something that's pre-programmed into our womanly little brains before we pop out into the world. Babies don't come out pink and blue; the world paints them that way. And along with ridiculous ideas like which colours you should and shouldn't like, we get the idea that it is 'girly' to worry about your weight, or that it's a typical 'woman thing' to ask, 'Does my bum look big in this?' But none of these ideas or worries actually come from inside us, they come from the world around us and the way we're taught to 'perform' being female, just as boys are taught to 'perform' being male.

The idea of what's 'girly' is helped along by toys and adverts, billboards and magazine covers, films and clothing. For example, here's a picture of some Monster High dolls a friend of mine owns.

They're aimed at girls aged around eight to twelve. They are wildly popular. Look at their bodies. Look at their legs. The same shape is repeated over and over, from Barbie to *TOPModel* magazine. It's how we're taught to want to look and we're taught it from a very young age. And somehow, along the way, we never stop to ask how weird it is that we don't know anyone who actually looks like a Monster High doll, or a Barbie. We just accept the idea that this thing we're supposed to strive for is mysteriously distant from our reality and, let's face it, unachievable.

How bizarre is that?

Imagine if, from an incredibly young age, we bombarded boys with dolls and images of men in magazines where they were all shaped like men but with really, weirdly large feet. Like absolutely *huge*, as if they're all walking round with canoes strapped to the bottoms of their ankles. And boys all grew up feeling like they had to pretend to have bigger feet, and they should always strive for bigger feet. So they'd wear shoes that were much too big for them with socks stuffed into the toes to pad them out, even though almost nobody in real life has feet that big. Wouldn't that seem ridiculous? But that's exactly what we do with the idea that girls should aspire to look like dolls who wouldn't even be able to stand up without falling over in real life!

In fact, there are a lot of double standards going on. Take women's body hair, for example. Armpit or leg hair is completely natural and even considered sexy on men, while it is somehow ugly and unforgivable and disgusting on women. WHY?

Of course boys face the same issues too, to a certain extent.

They too are being increasingly surrounded by images of tough, macho, muscly men and unattainable male beauty standards are also on the rise. We see David Beckham in his underwear on the sides of buses and David Gandy in his underwear on the front of magazines. But generally speaking, when we see the Davids in their underwear, it's because they're *selling* underwear. Other men in the public eye are often allowed to look older, or fatter, or shorter, or hairier than the 'ideal' male model. But for women, no matter why they are in the public eye, whether they're newsreaders, politicians or even on trial for murder (think Foxy Knoxy), we often see them being judged first and foremost on their looks, as if that's more important than anything else. Men can be themselves, but women have to be a sexier version of themselves. (Kind of like how men can dress up as a doughnut for Halloween, but if you're a woman you have to be a *sexy* doughnut).

The idea that there's one perfect way for all male and all female bodies to look isn't just harmful, it's downright stupid. We know how different we all are – that's what makes us so interesting and unique. So how strange it is to decide that there is one single cookie-cutter for men and one for women and we all just have to do our best to squeeze ourselves into it. What a weird idea.

But weird or not, it's incredibly powerful.

On a school visit recently, I handed out some worksheets to a group of twelve- to fourteen-year-olds. I asked them to draw a picture of themselves, and another of themselves with any changes they'd make, if they could, by waving a magic wand. The pictures the boys drew varied quite a lot. While some revealed that boys do worry about issues like building up muscles, others focused on more . . . *unusual* changes!

ME NOW

ME IF I COULD CHANGE ANYTHING

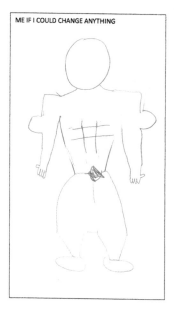

ME NOW

ME IF I COULD CHANGE ANYTHING

(That last one is my personal favourite, not only because he was so inventive about the qualities he'd like to add, but also because he totally embraced the fact that he has a carrot instead of a nose and didn't seem bothered about changing that at all.)

But the ones that came back from the girls showed the same change, again and again and again . . .

ME NOW

ME IF I COULD CHANGE ANYTHING

ME NOW

ME IF I COULD CHANGE ANYTHING

It doesn't seem to matter how old we are, what career we have, whether we're married, or religious, arty or musical or whatever. Women and girls, in their billions, are concerned with getting thin. I say *getting* thin, not *being* thin, because it feels like very, very few ever achieve that goal. I don't mean that nobody ever manages to lose weight. I mean that almost none of us feel like we've achieved that elusive goal of perfection. We might lose weight, but then we think we need to lose more. It's a constant process of disappointment, longing, loathing, relapse and self-punishment.

We can get past this. Repeat. We can get past this. This is not a drill.

I know this is going to sound incredibly simple, but I think it's the key:

The way you feel isn't linked to the shape of your body.

THE WAY YOU FEEL IS NOT LINKED TO THE SHAPE
OF YOUR BODY.

This is huge. This is important.

Behind all the obsession about women's bodies is the basic idea that losing weight and getting thinner will make us happier.

This is a massive lie.

How do I know?

Two reasons:

First: You might come across an old photograph of yourself and think: 'Wow. My body looked really great then, I wish I looked like that now.' But if you think back to how you felt about your body at that time, the chances are you had the same worries and insecurities back then too. Our bodies change but the way we feel about them doesn't. Whatever size we are, we tend to find things to worry about.

Second: I have lots of friends who look, to me, completely perfect. We've all been there – the friend whose flat stomach we eye enviously, or whose cellulite-free thighs we contemplate with secret sighs. It's very hard not to compare ourselves to those around us. To me, their bodies look exactly like the ones belonging to those girls in the magazines. But guess what? They're unhappy and worried about *their* bodies too. They have *other* friends whose arms they envy, or calves they prefer to their own. Probably one of those friends would prefer to have my boobs, or my hair . . . And so on forever, round and round in circles.

Having the 'perfect' body doesn't work as a magic solution to make you happy, because none of us will ever believe we have the perfect body. But if we could make ourselves believe it – not by changing our bodies, but changing the way we *think* about them . . . That just might work.

The problem with mentally mixing up your weight and your worth is that when you feel bad about your body, you value yourself less and start to assume everyone else will too. But we have to move away from the idea that our value, in other people's minds as well as our own, is based on the shape of our bodies and the way that we look. We *know* this isn't true. Think about it. Is your best friend the thinnest person you know? Are the people you most like and love exactly ranked in order of how much you like them, from thinnest to fattest, ugliest to prettiest? Of course they're not.

You're not an arsehole.

You judge people based on things like how nice, kind, funny and interesting they are, what they say and do, how they treat you and how you feel when you're with them. Why would anyone else behave any differently with you?

Just think how our poor bodies must feel, working away, doing what is frankly a pretty bloody miraculous job just keeping us alive and breathing and thinking, only to find us heaping hate on them at every opportunity.

Thighs: 'We would like to chip in here to say that we feel we get a particularly bad rep. We're constantly on the receiving end of criticism and dissatisfaction, but we are rarely ever praised, unless it's for getting as far away from each other as is humanly possible. Which is silly, because do you really want to go through life constantly doing the splits? Well, do you? We quite like each other and anyway we have to work together so we may as well rub along. Literally. We also feel like we perform a lot of awesome functions that go under-appreciated – like holding on to a moving bicycle, for example, not to mention a hot guy. If you had any idea how much work we do for you maybe you'd think twice about wanting to get rid of us, eh?'

In fact, we're so programmed to obsess over why we hate different parts of our body that we even have a vocabulary for it: 'problem areas'. We've seen too many 'circle of shame' and 'dress to flatter your figure' features. We start approaching our body parts as problems to cope with instead of joys to celebrate. The thighs are right. We rarely stop to think about the utterly awesome things our bodies do for us every single day.

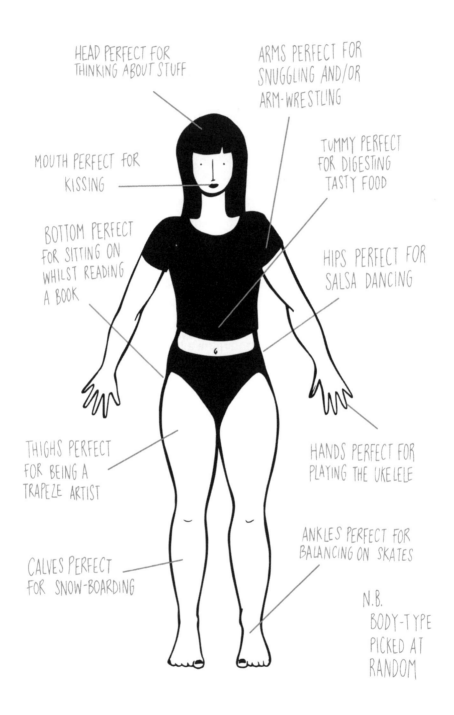

This doesn't mean I'm saying we shouldn't be healthy. There's a world of difference between the word 'healthy' and the word 'thin'. But our ideas about what is 'fat' or 'obese' are often so influenced by the world around us that we think we're overweight when we're healthy. Or we think a model's body is the most desirable way to look, when she might actually be so underweight that she's stopped having periods and isn't healthy at all. The best way to approach a healthy body is to take shape and size out of it altogether. There is no one healthy 'look'. People's healthy bodies all look different.

Our bodies tend to be healthiest when we eat sensibly and do a good amount of exercise. What does that mean? Well, luckily, our bodies are incredibly intelligent. Your body itself knows best, you just have to learn how to listen to it, and drown out all the other noise. Eat when you're hungry and stop when you're full. Don't starve yourself or force yourself to eat less than your body needs. Don't eat when you're not hungry. If you find this tricky, it's completely natural; after all, we have a lot of learned societal crap to cut through before we can work out what our bodies actually need. Learning about how to do this could fill a whole other book, and in fact it has: Susie Orbach has written more brilliantly and clearly on this topic than I ever could, and I really recommend her books on eating and bodies. You aren't what you eat. Your food is the fuel for all the amazingness you have to be getting on with! It doesn't define who you are any more than petrol makes a car into a Skoda or a Lamborghini! But we sometimes *use* food for different things – like emotional needs, unhappiness, or cravings. To work out if you are doing this, check in with your feelings when you eat. Are you eating because you're hungry, or is it really a hug or a chat you want? Are you eating to feel full or to feel in control? If you're eating when you're not really hungry, there might be other things that will better satisfy the urge you're actually feeling if you can work out what it is. Eating to manage anxiety or a low mood is common – eating slowly, thinking about and enjoying our food can help us to avoid that.

If you're really struggling with this, there is help available. Most of us experience body dissatisfaction, but for some it is part of a larger and more serious health problem. If you are worried, check out Beat (details in the back of the book).

Similar rules apply to exercise. Do what your body needs, not what society wants. Did you know that (according to Sport England) 2 million fewer women than men participate in sport and exercise regularly? Only 31 per cent of fourteen-year-old girls do regular exercise, compared to 50 per cent of boys the same age. And only 12 per cent of fourteen-year-old girls are getting *enough* exercise. But the weird thing is, it doesn't start out that way. In primary school, girls and boys are doing similar levels of activity, but the gap gets bigger and bigger as they get older ... why?[6]

There are lots of reasons, like school sport being skewed towards boys, or the media's failure to highlight the amazing female athletes out there. But research has found that one of the big factors putting young women off sport is the fear of looking sweaty and 'unfeminine', particularly in front of guys. Screw that!

Our concern with living up to the perfect feminine image is even affecting our health. And it just isn't worth it.

Remember that exercise should make you feel good, and it shouldn't be a punishment, or something you do excessively.

We need to work on accepting our bodies, and maybe even learning to love them.

I'm not saying you have to love your body all the time. That's just setting up another pressure that we can't all realistically live up to. But what we can try to do is, on the days that we worry about one or another bit of our body, remember that we are not defined by it. Our worth is not measured by a gap between our thighs. We are friends, daughters, sisters, lovers, listeners, talkers, thinkers, and a thousand other things that are not measured in centimetres or kilos. What we look like is not who we are. You aren't your body.

Learning to love your body isn't immediate. But what love is? (OK, yes, it is immediate with kittens.) Think about loving your body the way you love a person. Not necessarily a romantic lover, but a sibling, maybe, or a best friend. Your love for them builds gradually over time because of the time you spend together and everything you've been through. It takes time to really truly get to know them and love them for all their quirks. You don't love them for being the same as everybody else, you love them for their differences and what makes them truly unique. And it's not always easy to love them all the time – you're going to have fights and fallings out. But you accept them for who they are and you value them. All this is true with loving your body.

Don't expect a quick fix – it's a process.

This isn't easy. But it gets easier if we surround ourselves with things that help us to feel positive, and it's harder if we don't. There might be messages and conversations, from friends, peers or websites, that aren't very helpful and make us feel bad about our bodies. There might be people who are passing their own insecurities and worries onto you or taking them out on you. These are conversations we can choose to leave. They're websites we can choose not to visit.

Pretty much the strongest, most badass and rebellious thing that you can do is to love your body in this world that *screams* at you that you shouldn't. It's one of the ultimate ways to girl up.

I know that despite all this, despite the academic, logical reasoning, body confidence is nothing short of a full-pitched battle.

Or, more than that, it's a long series of battles in an ongoing war. There are a million tips and tricks out there, and different ones work for different people. What works on one day might not work the next. But when you find something that does work, use it. Hold onto it. Write it down. Because every battle you win brings you closer to winning the war. Here are a few techniques – they won't all work for you but hopefully one or two of them will be helpful weapons in your arsenal:

1. Stick together

Having supportive friends can make a world of difference when it comes to body confidence. Being around people who are constantly fat-shaming, or stressing about their weight can make you feel worried about yourself too. This doesn't mean you have to ditch your friends! But you can talk about the issues and make a decision as a group to try and be more body positive, to avoid 'fat talk' and to support one another in saying no to body image pressure.

2. Don't listen to magazines

Taking advice from magazines on body image is a bit like letting a drug dealer help you to get clean – their heart isn't in it! Want the perfect example? A few weeks ago, I followed a link to a list of 'Body Confidence Tips' in a 'Love Your Body' section on a well-known women's magazine website. No sooner had I read the first tip, than a pop-up appeared on my screen, blotting out the 'body confidence' advice with a huge advert offering a '21-Day Bikini Body Plan'.

Thanks for nothing.

3. Remember that you're not alone

The internet is bursting with incredible body confidence blogs, campaigns, Tumblrs and Instagrams and they can really work. I've met a lot of teenage girls who've found them life-changing. If thin, airbrushed, identical women are the wallpaper of your life then change it by introducing yourself to some of these beacons of utter awesomeness. (Check out the Fuck Yeah Body Image, Stop Hating Your Body and Halt the Body Hate Tumblrs)

4. Somebody who loves you won't want to change you

Since a lot of the media hype around our bodies focuses on the idea of using them to snare the perfect guy, it's natural that a lot of body anxiety can be about whether or not a potential partner will find you attractive. But think about the different people you've had crushes on. Did they all have exactly the same body and face? (If so, I don't mean to alarm you but I think you might be dealing with a cloning situation . . . run, run as fast as you can and don't look back.) We don't fall for people because of their bodies in real life, we fall for who they are and their body comes as part of that. Somebody who really likes you, and deserves your time and company, isn't going to be judging you based on the pieces of you that digest your food or get you from A to B. They'll care about you, just the way you are.

And finally, in the battle against these dark arts of advertising, media and fashion, remember that they fight dirty. Remember that the images we see aren't even real. Remember that they have the dastardly weapon of airbrushing at their disposal and they aren't afraid to use it.

It's one thing to talk about airbrushing in theory, but sometimes you just have to see it for yourself to truly grasp the extent to which these images we see every day have been manipulated. I wanted to see how much of a difference it made, so I dug out my bikini, screwed up my courage and sent my picture to a digital airbrushing artist. You know what I discovered?

AIRBRUSHING
is...

... a

MASSIVE

lie

Now, I know this will be a difficult question to answer, but I want you to look carefully at these two pictures and see if you can work out which one is airbrushed. What's that? You need more time? I totally understand. I realize it's pretty difficult to work out.

Just look at the difference! Just look at the pieces they've hacked off and sawn away and hoovered out. What's wrong with a birthmark, for cripes sake? Why don't I need that piece of armpit? How are my bikini bottoms supposed to stay on without the bits of hip that were holding them up? What is it about women's bodies that's so offensive we have to pick and scrape away at them until they practically disappear?

The funny thing is I thought the second picture looked pretty great before I saw the airbrushed version. It's only when you compare the two that it makes the second one look 'worse'. That's what airbrushing does. It moves the goalposts. It sets up reality against fake female perfection so none of us can ever win.

But the most important thing about the second picture is my smile. I'm smiling because I'm happy, and how happy I am isn't connected to my body, just like who I am and what I'm worth isn't defined by the firmness of my stomach or the size of my thighs. There's nothing to hide. Your body isn't who you are but it sure is coming with you everywhere you go, and you're in it together for the long haul, so you might as well get to know and appreciate it for its own value, not anybody else's.

CHAPTER THREE

MAKING WAVES

We teach boys that it's sexy for them to make demands and decisions. We teach boys it's hot for them to be in control. We teach girls that it's cute to be coy and a little bit helpless. We show them girls in films who are slightly confused and occasionally fall over their own shoelaces, and win all the boys' hearts with their kooky, awkward klutziness.

You know what I'm talking about.

Kooky Klutz Level 1: Burst into a meeting that you're not meant to be at but look RIDICULOUSLY sexy/kittenish/ erotic while doing it.

Kooky Klutz Level 2: Accidentally get a smudge of flour on your nose while baking adorable cupcakes.

Kooky Klutz Level 3: Misunderstand maths, but in a really delightful way so that some handsome, slightly patronising guy can fall in love with you while teaching you how to do it.

Kooky Klutz Level 4: Have a dog but don't be quite strong enough to be able to take it for a walk without it pulling you along and do this in a flimsy dress.

Kooky Klutz Level 5: Don't be that great at your job so a guy can come and rescue you.

Kooky Klutz Level 1000: Fall into a cake. Still look ravishing. Lick it off seductively.

This also extends into adulthood – look at these different characteristics and how differently we interpret them depending on the sex of the person who exhibits them:

Characteristic	Man	Woman
Takes the lead	Authoritative	Bossy
Speaks loudly	Charismatic	Shrill
Commands others	Leader	Ballbreaker
Argues their corner	Firm	Abrasive
Pushes the point	Persistent	Nagging
Expressive	In touch with his emotions	Hormonal
Animated	Passionate	Hysterical
Affectionate	Loving	Clingy

You get the point.

The trouble is, girls end up at the bottom of the pile when it comes to authority. We are trained not to use our voices, taught only about being good and polite and accommodating and told not to bother anybody.

But this is an unrealistic and ineffective method of doing business. Imagine where we'd be today if the incredible women who campaigned for equal pay had gone:

WHAT DO WE WANT?
EQUAL PAY!
WHEN DO WE WANT IT?
giggles and runs away

We'd be many thousands of pounds per year worse off, that's where.

The unequal treatment of girls by those in authority is so normalized you might not even notice it at first. But it's the small, subtle things that you start to see. The way that a brother or male cousin is allowed out later than you, or permitted to go somewhere that's 'too dangerous' for you to go as a girl. The way the guys can be loud and boisterous because 'boys will be boys' but girls are shushed and shut down and expected to keep themselves neat and tidy and not bother anyone. Being told you can't wear certain things 'because of the way people will look at you' when guys get to wear whatever they want. The way that the boys often sit back and relax at home while the girls help with the cooking, or clear the table. The times when girls are expected to be sensible, or responsible, or hard-working and guys seem to get a free pass. The incidents where a guy hounds a girl and grabs her or chases her, but when she pushes him away, *she* gets into trouble.

According to the *Daily Mirror,* at a school in Wales, a girl was being taunted by sexist boys telling her to get back in the kitchen and make them a sandwich. When she finally lost her temper and swore at them, the school banned *her* from going on a school trip to a theme park, while the boys weren't punished at all. (Luckily her totally awesome mum made her a 'F@*K Sexism' T-shirt and drove her to the theme park anyway.)

It doesn't happen all the time and it doesn't happen to everybody. But when it does, it's beyond infuriating.

Sometimes challenging these things can help other people

recognize that they're unfair too – for example, some parents might not realize that there's an unfair division of labour going on at home until you point it out. Maybe it was like that in their house when they grew up and they've just carried on without thinking about it.

Pointing things out isn't easy, especially because people don't always respond the way you'd like them to. People may react defensively, especially if it feels like you're criticising them. They might deny that there's a problem, or try to defend themselves by justifying it. To deal with these actions, it helps to be prepared.

If you're planning to challenge authority, whether with your parents or at school or university, make sure you arm yourself with information. If you're questioning the fact that girls in your house seem to do a lot more housework than boys, don't just go ahead and say it, wait a month and write down every household chore you do and every one your brothers do and then use it to show your parents the evidence. If you're challenging your school or university about a problem, write down every time it happens and note the names of other people who were present so you can prove it's really an issue.

And above all, remember, in pretty much any situation, it's always OK to ask 'why?'

Why do I have to do that? Why can't I go there? Why am I the one being asked to change? Why is that the rule? (The only circumstance I can think of where this wouldn't apply would be if you were trapped in a room with a bomb on a timer and the bomb disposal expert is on the phone talking you through how to diffuse it and telling you which wires to cut. Probably best not to ask why in that situation.)

Rules should have reasons – if they're sensible, then they should be able to stand up to a bit of questioning. And if a rule doesn't have a good reason, if it's just 'because I said so', then why should you be expected to follow it?

Obviously I'm not saying you should never follow instructions, or giving you a carte blanche to be rude! But if girls throughout history had always accepted the rules and restrictions that were placed on them because it was 'just the way things are' or 'because I said so' or 'because you're a girl', we might still be sitting at home knitting socks for the men, with no money or property of our own, no right to work and really, *really* unfulfilling sex lives.

Women and girls who challenged authority and broke down barriers are to thank for a *helluva* lot of progress in our lives, and they have charted a long and noble history of having no fucks to give for stupid or sexist forms of authority.

For example, in the 1880s, when Nellie Bly was a teenager, her local paper, the *Pittsburgh Dispatch,* printed a nasty and misogynistic column called 'What are girls good for'. Nellie thought so little of the column that she wrote her own angry anonymous response. In a long and noble tradition of historical men who saw historical women challenging authority and completely lost their shit, the editor literally didn't know what to do about this. So he took out a full-page advertisement promising a job to the author if they came forward. Bly answered the ad and became a journalist, focusing on social justice and reporting on political corruption. But her editors tried to force her to write only about fashion and flower shows, for which Nellie simply had no fucks to give, so she left them a note and moved to New York, aged twenty-three. She went on to pioneer investigative journalism, raise awareness of the conditions in mental hospitals and sweat shops, and famously became the first woman to travel around the world in seventy-two days, with only £200, a few pairs of knickers and absolutely zero fucks about her person.

*

Gertrude Bell was born in 1868. She eventually became known as the female Lawrence of Arabia, because the best way people could think of to honour an amazing woman was to compare her to a man. Most girls of the time weren't highly educated, so she became one of the first women to study at Oxford University, achieving first class honours. Then she became an explorer, a spy, an advisor to the British government and a general all-round legend. Giving no fucks at all for sexist norms or a sore bottom, she travelled thousands of miles across the desert by camel, financed her own archaeological expeditions when nobody would pay for a woman to do them and spent many hours hanging off a mountain by a rope when one of her climbing escapades went wrong. Then she put two fingers up to colonialism and helped protect Iraq's control over its archaeological treasures. She also drafted an important report on Mesopotamia, but got understandably peeved when people were more shocked by the fact that it was written by a woman than its contents. She wrote to her parents: 'I hope they'll drop that source of wonder and pay attention to the report itself, if it will help them to understand what Mesopotamia is like.' Later she may or may not have added: 'P.S. I have no fucks to give at all for those idiots.'

✳

Eighteenth-century Frenchwoman Emilie du Châtelet ignored her mother's pleas for her to enjoy more 'ladylike' pursuits like gossiping about clothes and studied Latin, Greek and maths instead, then used her mad skills to cheat at cards so she could buy more books. She started working on scientific theory with Voltaire, but naturally he fell in love with her and then got his feelings hurt when she turned out to be better at science than him, so he went off in a strop. Having zero fucks to give for his childishness, she told him it was ridiculous to think that an intelligent woman like her would need a man to be happy. After her death her important scientific work came to play a major role in the development of energy theories, but nobody really believed a woman could have come up with them because patriarchy, so she was largely written out of the history books.

＊

Aged about thirteen, Hillary Rodham quite fancied a career as an astronaut so (like a total boss) she wrote to NASA to ask how to make it happen. NASA replied that they weren't really interested in female astronauts. Having not one solitary fuck to give for that answer, she decided to become Secretary of State and stand for president instead. Now she's kind of a big deal, and will probably be refusing to give any funding to NASA when she's president unless they girl up and get 50:50 men and women flying each and every spacecraft. Kinda would have been easier to have just given her a job in the first place.

＊

Clara Barton was born in 1821 and never, at any stage, gave a single fuck. She outraged everybody by not only playing with her male cousins, but being just as good if not better than them at everything, which basically made everybody faint with horror. Her mother panicked and invited one of her female cousins over to help teach her how to be feminine, for which Clara probably gave absolutely no fucks whatsoever. Aged about ten she taught herself how to care for her brother after he was injured in a fall and continued to nurse him with medicine and leeches long after doctors had given up, leading him to make a full recovery. This was just the first of a tediously long list of times men tried to tell Clara she was wrong before she turned around and made them look foolish.

She started teaching in her teens and later set up the first free school in New Jersey. Probably stunned by the horror of a woman doing an actual job, the chaps in charge gave her a completely unsuitable warehouse space and only a handful of kids turned up on her first day. Because she didn't have any kitchen facilities, she had to send the children home at lunchtime and thought they might not come back. That afternoon there were three times as many students. By the end of her first year, she'd only gone and increased the school to 603 pupils. So what did those clever men do? They decided such a big school needed a man to run it and hired a headmaster instead. Being a total frickin' badass she declared: 'I may sometimes be willing to teach for nothing, but if paid at all, I shall never do a man's work for less than a man's pay' (she later added 'because I have literally not one fuck to give for that'.) So she packed her bags and went and got a job in the US Patent Office, where she casually acquired the first ever salary that was equal to a man's because she was Clara bloody Barton. But could they see how much of a good thing she was? Could they heck. Her job was downgraded and eventually eliminated because of opposition to women working in government offices, for which Clara gave precisely zero fucks.

Then the Civil War started, so naturally she wanted to go and serve on the front line, and I will give you one single guess what the answer was to that. Not really one to be defeated, she set about gathering supplies for the troops and amassed several whole warehouses full of gear. Then she went and told the leaders of the Northern campaign they could only have the stuff if they let her go to the front line and they were like 'yeah, OK'. Weirdly, at no point does anyone seem to have said, 'Hey guys, let's stop being douchecanoes and just listen to this girl who has literally proved us wrong. Every. Single. Time.'

Anyway, Clara completely kicked ass in the war, working on the front line, tending to men while bullets zipped so close to her they made holes in her sleeves, and generally being such a badass she was literally put in charge of all the hospitals. (At which stage the guys who didn't want to let her go to the front line in the first place were like #AWKWARD).

Later she founded the American Red Cross, even though it took her many years to persuade the presidents of the time that the US would ever need it, since they thought the country would never face another calamity like the recently ended Civil War. Sadly she died in 1912, narrowly missing the outbreak of the First World War and the opportunity to send the president a brief but satisfying telegram saying: 'See?'

✳

If you're looking to join in smashing boundaries, giving zero fucks and standing up to authority a little closer to home than the early 1900s, there is a revolution going on across several different countries at the moment, where young people, particularly young women, are rising up to protest against sexist and unfair dress codes.

There is major hypocrisy going on here. I'm not saying nobody should be asked to dress smartly for school or college, but it feels like there's some sexism going into people's ideas about what 'smart' looks like. Some schools freak out about seeing girls' upper arms, or shoulders, or knees, while nobody is having heart palpitations about seeing those bits of boys' bodies. Adult (and sexist) ideas about what bits of women's bodies are seen as 'sexualized' are projected onto the bodies of teenage girls whether they like it or not. At lots of schools, while girls are told they should cover up to avoid distracting the boys, boys who harass and even grope girls are excused with the line 'boys will be boys'.

One pupil tweeted me to say she'd been told her skirt was too short ... on the same day a boy in her class was wearing a T-shirt emblazoned with a picture of a naked woman.

Another girl wrote to the Everyday Sexism Project saying: 'I got dress-coded at my school for wearing shorts. After I left the principal's office with a detention I walked past another student wearing a shirt depicting two stick figures: the male holding down the female's head in his crotch and saying "good girls swallow". Teachers walked right past him and didn't say a thing.'

At one school a girl in jeans and a long-sleeved cardigan was sent home because her outfit revealed her ...

DRUMROLL ....

....

COLLARBONE!!!!

(Clara Barton frequently came up against this exact same problem. In 1840.)

A school in the UK banned girls from wearing tight trousers in case they made male staff feel 'uncomfortable'. Another sent home 150 girls on the first day of term because their skirts were a smidgen shorter than the required number of inches, but nobody was lining up with a ruler to check anything about the boys' appearance. A high school in Manhattan faced protests from students after implementing a new dress code that reportedly included a ban on showing shoulders. Girls at a junior high school in California were taken aside and told they couldn't wear trousers that were 'too tight' for fear of distracting the boys. In Minnesota, a high school principal sent parents an email asking them to prevent girls from wearing tight-fitting leggings or yoga trousers because they could 'be highly distracting for other students'.

At one high school in California, forty female students were sent home from a dance after apparently being forced to twirl and flap their arms up and down as male staff inspected their attire. (Yep, like chickens. In. Real. Life.)

The codes aren't only problematic for sexist reasons. A student at one school I visited explained that the dress code didn't take different body shapes into account, making it much harder for her to conform to standards of what was considered 'respectable' than some of her friends, who were naturally less curvaceous, even while wearing the same clothes.

And one girl's Everyday Sexism Project entry read: 'At age ten

I was pulled out of my fifth grade class for a few minutes for a "special health lesson". As an early bloomer, I already had obvious breasts and was the tallest in my class. I thought they were giving me a paper about reproductive health that's normally given to the twelve-year-old girls. Instead I was told to cover my body more because I was different.'

Similar incidents have seen boys targeted or banned from school for wearing traditionally 'feminine' fashion, from skinny jeans to skirts, make-up to wigs. A transgender student said he was threatened with having his photo barred from the school yearbook simply because he chose to wear a tuxedo to prom. A twelve-year-old African-American girl was threatened with expulsion for refusing to cut her natural afro hair. School administrators told her mother she violated school dress codes for being 'a distraction'.

Which all leads to several big questions:

- Are we saying girls' bodies are dangerous and sexual, even if they themselves don't choose to see them in that way?

- Are we really saying that boys can't control themselves and girls are responsible for covering up because otherwise the guys won't be able to help themselves from looking/harassing/groping? Come on now.

- If a male teacher is 'distracted' by the shoulders or knees of an underage pupil, is she really the problem here?

- Who is being 'protected' and why?

- What social norms and stereotypes are being reinforced and is it the role of a school to reinforce or to challenge them?

- When they said the tight trousers made male teachers feel uncomfortable, was it because they were trying to wear them?

- Are we making it a rule-breaking offence to be different?

- Doesn't this all seem pretty unfair?

If this is an uprising you want to be part of, you need to start by working out whether there is a problem ...

A QUICK GUIDE: HOW TO TELL IF A DRESS CODE IS SEXIST

- Count up the number of rules: are there more about girls' clothing than boys'?

- Is the level of body exposure the same for girls and for boys? (If boys can show shoulders, or knees, or thighs, why shouldn't girls be able to as well?)

- Look at the reasons given: does the code state that girls need to avoid 'distracting' or 'embarrassing' boys or male teachers? Does it refer to a 'distraction-free' learning environment?

- Does the dress code decree that certain parts of girls' bodies (knees, thighs, shoulders, upper arms, backs) or clothing (bra straps) are sexual or 'inappropriate'?

- If your school has a uniform, are girls banned from wearing trousers while boys are allowed to?

- How is the dress code enforced? Are girls more

frequently pulled up and punished than boys for dress-code infringements?

- Do girls miss lesson time because they are sent home, sent to change or sent out of class for wearing the wrong clothing and/or 'distracting' the boys?

- Are girls humiliated or publicly shamed for dress-code violations, by being forced to wear something embarrassing, for example?

- How does the dress code relate to other issues – for example, are boys less strictly disciplined for harassing girls than girls are for breaking the dress code?

If the answer to one or more of the above questions is 'yes' then you may be dealing with a sexist dress code.

The first thing to know is that you are not alone.

The good news is, a lot of other girls think it's unfair too, and they're not taking it lying down. Here are some brilliant tips you can learn from real-life students who have stood up to their schools, on a number of different issues.

POINT OUT THE HYPOCRISY

The school that banned leggings and yoga trousers, telling students the dress code was designed to prevent boys from being 'distracted', saw the girls show up in leggings to protest against the sexist policy. They held big signs that said: 'Are my trousers lowering your test scores?'

ENLIST ALLIES

When a seventeen-year-old transgender student in Brazil was fined for coming to school wearing a skirt, her male classmates showed their support by all coming into school wearing skirts. Unable to fine the entire student body, the school was forced to revise its code instead.

BEAT THEM AT THEIR OWN GAME

In one case, students fighting to be allowed to start a Gay-Straight Alliance club at their high school were able to insist it should be allowed (over protests from the school board) because a conservative state senator had previously sponsored legislation demanding equal access for extracurricular clubs in order to allow Bible study clubs in schools!

KNOW YOUR RIGHTS

In the UK, the section of the Equality Act 2010 which relates to schools states that a school must not discriminate against, harass or victimize a pupil on grounds of any protected characteristic, including sex. And in the United States, the federal Title IX statute prohibits sex discrimination in education. Under both these requirements, if it can be proved that a school's dress code, for example, disproportionately and unfairly targeted girls, it could be suggested that the school is breaking the law. And these laws don't just protect girls' rights – in fact a legal case in Chicago challenged a school for discriminating against boys by mandating that they had to keep their hair cut short while girls were allowed to grow theirs long. When boys are bullied for wanting to wear nail varnish, or ridiculed for choosing something pink, they're suffering from the same rigid ideas about what it means to be a girl or a boy and how we should express that in our outward appearance. Gender stereotypes limit us all.

REVENGE CAN BE A DISH BEST SERVED COLD

One kick-ass teenager, Chloe Cross, waited until she graduated and simply printed this as her yearbook quote: 'I would just like to apologize to those who were unable to graduate with the class of 2015 because they were too distracted by my midriff and consequently failed all of their classes! Xoxo.' Burn.

USE SOCIAL MEDIA

Students protesting unfair school dress codes have recently drawn international attention to the issue using the hashtag #IAmMoreThanADistraction This highlights the problem, puts pressure on schools to shape up and allows students to share strategies for successful protest.

Speaking of which . . .

A QUICK GUIDE: HOW TO ORGANIZE A PROTEST

Whether you're protesting about dress codes or any other issue you feel passionate about, there are lots of different forms of protest, including outdoor rallies or marches, stunts, flashmobs, days of action, online campaigns, hashtags, chalk walks, pickets, sit-ins, occupations, petitions and letter campaigns.

The very first thing to do is to set out clearly what it is you are protesting. You need to be able to explain concisely and plainly what the problem is and what you want to change. What would be your ideal outcome? What do you want to see happen? Be realistic. ('Cats creep me out', 'No More Mondays' or 'Ban All the Cheese' are unlikely to be successful campaigns, no matter how strongly you feel.)

The second thing to do is to work out which type of protest will be most effective for a particular problem. You wouldn't want to hold a sit-in to campaign against uncomfortable chairs. Sometimes it might work to combine different kinds of protest – like an online campaign supported by a rally, or a petition which uses a hashtag and social media account to raise awareness of what is going on.

Third, you need to identify who is in a position to make the change happen. Is it an individual, a politician, a company, or a school board? Once you have this clear, work out what the best method is to target them. Who influences them? Who are they answerable to? If they are an elected official, they may be influenced by a petition with signatories from their constituency. If they are a public figure, they may be persuaded by an open letter that attracts attention. If they are a big company, they may respond to media attention, not wanting to attract negative publicity.

Before you go any further, the fourth step is to prepare for potential road bumps ahead. What might happen when you launch your protest? Do you need to make preparations in advance? If you plan to rally, flashmob or march outside, you may need to get permission in advance from police or local authorities. Remember you may need extra permission to use speakers or loud hailers. Make sure anybody who is going to attend understands your parameters for a peaceful protest and agrees to abide by them. If you are planning to campaign online, there is always a chance you might attract some unwanted attention. Take steps to protect your online accounts, including strong, different passwords for each account, and lock down permissions on your social media pages and photographs. Use a web search like Pipl or My Reputation to check that your personal contact details are not freely available online to avoid trolling or 'doxxing' (a kind of attack where somebody's personal details such as an address or phone number are spread online to incite harassment).

Fifth, work out how you're going to publicize your protest. You want to make noise for two reasons: firstly because you need lots of people to join in to help make your protest successful, and secondly because publicity can help hold people to account and force your target to respond to your protest. The web makes it easy to spread the word – you can create a website, a Facebook event page, a Twitter feed or a Tumblr for your protest and invite people to participate. Remember other forms of media too, like writing an article in your school or university newspaper, your local paper or even the national press. Printed T-shirts can be another great way to remind people about your campaign and keep them talking about it – go for large font and not too much information, so they can be easily read at a distance. (The 'No More Page 3' T-shirts are a great example.) Are there email lists or local radio stations that you could approach to help you get the word out?

Sixth, make it easy for people to join you. If you are using a website, or posters, or flyers, make sure they prominently and simply outline what it is you want people to *do*. Whether it is writing a letter, using a hashtag, or signing a petition, make sure it's clear at every stage how people can get involved.

Seventh, unite with other groups. Search out organizations with similar aims and ask them to come on board, both to add weight to your campaign and to help you spread the word further.

Eighth, escalate! If your campaign hasn't been effective, consider how you can up the ante. Add in new forms of protest from the list, like a rally or petition, or think about involving the media if it might help elicit a positive response.

Ninth, negotiate success. Be prepared that when you get a response it may not be everything you'd hoped for. If you're offered a compromise, you'll need to think carefully and consult with the people who have supported your campaign to work out what looks like success, and whether a compromise is worth it.

Tenth, follow up. It can be easy for organizations or groups to cave in to the pressure of a protest and then wait for all the publicity to die away and not make the changes they promised. Make sure you follow up and see that the changes you agreed are implemented, sooner rather than later.

Modern young women are using these techniques and more to fight back against authority, and they are winning! And it's not just about dress codes either.

For example, two Canadian thirteen-year-olds, Tessa Hill and Lia Valente, launched a 'Change.org' petition calling on the Ontario Ministry of Education to include the topic of sexual consent on the school curriculum. 40,900 signatures, a viral short film and a meeting with the Premier of Ontario later, they'd secured a promise to put consent on the curriculum.

You have the right to have a say in the ideas and beliefs that are presented to you at school and like Hill and Valente, you have every right to challenge them.

In the UK, it's not currently compulsory for schools to teach anything about consent or healthy relationships, only about the actual biology of sex. At some schools, you're lucky even to get the hopelessly outdated old condom-on-a-banana trick. This is something you could challenge, by asking your school or university to teach young people about these issues and explaining why they are so important. A recent study by the National Union of Students found that only half of universities audited had a formal policy on sexual harassment – another major issue that you could campaign on.[1]

Challenging authority isn't always easy. This can be particularly true when it feels like sexism, or a lack of understanding of your choices, sexuality or gender identity, is coming from within your own family. It really hurts when the people who don't seem to understand are the people you love.

One of the things that might help is to check out how other people have dealt with similar situations. There are a lot of great places you can go online to read about other young people's experiences, strategies and coping mechanisms, which might help you work out how you want to approach a situation. (There are some good starting points in the back of the book.)

Whether you're thinking about coming out to your family or trying to talk to them about problems you are facing, remember that parents are human too. They might say hurtful or prejudiced things but it might be because they are a product of their own upbringing, or they may have never examined their attitudes towards a particular topic. They might have simply picked up society's default position. It might not be what they really believe, deep down. It doesn't necessarily mean they wouldn't be open to having a conversation and learning more. Often, prejudice comes from a place of ignorance and fear. There are brilliant organizations out there to provide support and information, like Families and Friends of Lesbians and Gays, Mermaids UK and Being Gay Is Okay (details in the back of the book).

It is important to know that if you are struggling, you aren't alone and there are helplines and support organizations you can talk to, who can help you work through what you are facing and let you know what your options are. Your safety and emotional well-being should always come first.

When it comes to protests and petitions, you also must remember that challenging authority is a risk, and it doesn't always work out the way you'd planned. (This isn't a disclaimer! Though please don't do anything awful and blame it on this book, OK thanks bye.)

Alongside all those amazing people who did challenge authority and successfully change things, there are hundreds of others whose names we don't know, because their efforts were suppressed, or they lived in a time too early for their open-mindedness and insight to be accepted. But just because we don't write about them in the history books doesn't mean for one moment that their efforts and protests were in vain. Nobody can fix a problem the very first time they come up against it. If it's a truly major issue, it's going to take years of patient and frustrating hard work to chip away and make progress. Each one of those people who does end up in the history books is standing on the shoulders of the hundreds who came before them and paved the way for their success. If you try to challenge unfair or prejudiced authority and find that you aren't successful, it doesn't mean you've failed. It means you've played a part in a revolution whose end just isn't yet in sight. And even if you manage to make one person think differently, or change one single mind, you've taken a step towards a goal that will eventually be reached, thanks to your help. Winning isn't everything. Making a difference is what matters.

CHAPTER FOUR

'MEAN GIRLS' AND MENTAL HEALTH

A few months after I started Everyday Sexism, I was asked to go and give a talk to the King's College London feminist society about gender inequality and sexual harassment. I'd never done anything like it before and the idea of speaking to a room full of about thirty students was terrifying. I didn't sleep at all the night before, and on the bus on the way there, with shaking hands, I dialled my sister and told her I didn't think I could go through with it. Very calmly, she told me if I was nervous I should just imagine the audience in their underwear. Very hysterically, I replied that that would be *extremely* inappropriate given the content of my talk. Somehow she managed to calm me down enough to girl up and proceed to the venue, instead of jumping off the bus and running all the way home. This is how I imagined the talk would go:

I arrive, slip over and immediately fall flat on my face (in the awkward, earth-please-swallow-me-whole way, not the dainty, Jennifer

Lawrence, how-did-I-somehow-just-become-even-cooler-by-falling-down way). I get up to talk but realize that I no longer speak English and my notes have caught fire. I try to put them out using the glass of water kindly provided for me, but lose my grip, throwing both water and glass into the face of the nearest Femsoc member, which breaks her nose. I try to distract from the fire and the blood by pulling up my first PowerPoint slide, but have accidentally mixed up my sexism statistics slides with photos I sent to the vet when my cat had a leaking anus. The Femsoc students are so disgusted by my presentation that they've decided women actually *are* the weaker sex and they've renamed it Misogyny Soc and started reaching out to other universities up and down the country to take the same step. Germaine Greer, Emmeline Pankhurst's great-granddaughter and the ghost of Simone de Beauvoir arrive in giant dancing vagina costumes to ceremonially excommunicate me from feminism and tell me I have set the movement back so far it's actually worse than when we started.

This is how the talk actually went:

For the first ten minutes, my mouth felt like sandpaper and I rattled through my facts so fast the poor students probably had no idea what I was on about. But gradually, I started to realize that time was passing and nobody had thrown vegetables at me and run screaming from the room. Nobody had protested, or shouted at me to please for the love of God stop talking. Nothing had spontaneously combusted – neither my notes nor, contrary to popular belief, my bra.

I started to relax and dared to actually glance up from my notecards occasionally. People seemed to be nodding. At one point they even laughed. *With* me, not *at* me!!! At the end of the talk, I handed out a brief survey and a really nice person came up and pointed out, in a friendly way, that she disagreed with something I'd written. She was right. I learned something.

It went OK.

A couple of weeks later I was asked to do another talk to a slightly bigger room of students and I felt ever so slightly less nervous. Then the next one, and the next, and so on, until I found that I could actually sleep before doing a talk, and that occasionally I'd mix up my words and correct myself and the whole world didn't fall down.

Even when I really stumbled and lost my place, everything was sort of OK. I mean, it wasn't *great*, obviously, but the world didn't explode and there were no locusts or tennis ball-size hailstones or rivers of blood.

The reason I'm telling you all this is because it represents some helpful life lessons I wish I'd learned sooner (along with: 'if you boogie board in a bikini your breasts WILL make a bid for freedom', which most people learn the hard way, so it's a really great piece of advice to get early).

The lessons are:

1. Sometimes we focus so much on the worst that could happen that it holds us back from doing things that could be amazing. Really, even if the very worst does happen, things are usually OK. You can't let fear stop you doing things, otherwise you'll never do anything at all, and doesn't that sound even scarier in the long run?

2. You can take it one step at a time. On that first day, as I practically had a heart attack over addressing thirty students, if someone had told me I would be speaking at the United Nations the following year I would have been like: 'uh-uh, no way, noooope, I'm out'. I never, ever would have thought I could do it. But doing a little bit at a time, practising over and over, talking to slightly bigger groups each time, I gradually reached a point where talking in front of people felt like no biggie at all. By the time I reached the UN I wasn't even nervous. And I never, ever thought I would type that sentence.

3. Ghosts don't exist.

I wish I'd learned some of this sooner, because early on in life is when you could really use this kind of info, particularly when it comes to fears of public humiliation (and ghosts). School and university are particularly strange places, because people are still working out who they are and what they want, and it all happens in a big cross between a microscope and a pressure cooker where everyone wants to know everyone else's business and there's a great deal of importance placed on who is and isn't cool.

The important thing to know is that the rest of the world isn't like this. Outside educational institutions, the concept of 'cool' largely disappears. Honestly.

But in the meantime, it's easy to get caught up in the system of hierarchy and points and reputation. People can give away your secrets and betray your trust. Friends can suddenly seem to change sides for no apparent reason at all. There's a 'currency' in joining in the teasing or making fun of somebody who is a common target, because people feel a relief that they're not the person being picked on. The easiest way to avoid being the person who's bullied is to be the bully yourself. That's why a lot of bullies have worries and insecurities about themselves, and turn them on other people to make themselves feel better. That's why it's so easy for a crowd to laugh along with a bully and so difficult for anyone to stand up to them.

But here's the thing – when you actually stop and think about what the things are that we bully people for, they're actually not that embarrassing at all. They're usually pretty normal, in fact. When did we decide that it's shameful to drop your tray at lunch? Or hugely embarrassing to be a different size or shape from someone else? Or run at a different speed? Or speak in a different way? What strange things to get hung up on, when you think about it.

If you come across this kind of behaviour while you're young, at school, or college, know that it won't be like this for ever. You will leave these small institutions behind and find that the world outside really is a bigger, brighter, and generally far less mean place.

Even more importantly, you will look back and realize that the things you were most teased for may well turn out to be the things that made you stand out and shine. And the people teasing you were wishing they had some of that. And you might even be glad of the exact things you were made to feel were embarrassing or stupid.

There are so many different ways to shine. You might shine because you are not afraid to be different. You might shine because you are very smart, or funny, or kind, very good at reading, or drawing, or swimming, or doing woodwork, or being a good friend, or writing songs. The way you shine isn't always the accepted way to be. And the brighter you shine, the more other people can sense it. There are other people around you who might not shine very bright, and the least shiny of them know, somewhere, in some deep, sad part of them, that very soon you will outshine them. And it's hard to feel that way, so they'll try to dim your light.

That's what bullying is. It is people who feel worried about the brightness of their own flame trying hard to blow out yours. People who feel threatened or scared by your light and colour and brightness, trying to snuff it out to help them feel less sad and less alone.

The awful thing is that knowing this doesn't necessarily make you feel any better at the time. The awful thing is that it can be really hard to believe that there's any light in you anywhere. The awful thing is that the bully often has other people on their side.

But the wonderful part is that your light isn't so easy to put out. It might flicker, or even seem to be extinguished for a while, but it's there and it will burn bright again. Good friends are the ones who hold their hand around your flame when other people are trying to blow it out.

Kindness shines brightest of all.

Try to remember this when things feel hard. It will get better. And it's much better in the end to be the person with the brightest, shiniest flame, even if it falters for a while, than to be the person who will always only have a flicker to light them through the dark.

WEIRD THINGS ABOUT POPULARITY

- It doesn't really mean anything, but we care about it a lot.
- Justin Bieber is really popular.
- Also cronuts. What is wrong with you people?
- The people who are really showy – Cool kids with a capital 'C' – at school very rarely go on to be big successes in later life. Not only do they basically peak too soon, but they also miss out on the chance to learn the vital life skills like self-deprecation, resilience and creating imaginary friends that help lead to success later on. (Albert never stops believing in me, do you Albert?)

TRUTHS ABOUT POPULARITY

- In the long run, the nicest people end up waaaay more popular.
- Popularity can't be bought, it's about how you treat people.
- Popularity means being friends with as many people as possible, not just the ones who make you look good, and definitely not the ones who want to exclude other people.
- Emma Watson, Millie Mackintosh, Jennifer Lawrence, Tyra Banks, Demi Lovato and Selena Gomez are just a few of the very successful and popular people who have described being bullied at school. So clearly being bullied says a lot more about the bully than it does about you.

WAYS TO DEAL WITH UNCOMFORTABLE MOMENTS WHEN YOU FEEL UNPOPULAR OR AWKWARD

E.G.: Waiting to be picked for teams; sitting on your own on the bus when others are sitting together; walking through the dining hall at lunchtime looking for someone to sit with; being on school trips when they let you go off into Doncaster for free time with £5 pocket money and you don't have an obvious group to go with; being in the playground and trying to get in on a game without it looking forced; waiting to meet someone and they haven't got there yet and people think you've been stood up even though you haven't (or whatever, maybe they got the date wrong); being the first to arrive for a lesson and you're sitting in the room alone when others arrive in pairs and groups; and eating in a restaurant alone. What do you mean I have a suspiciously high number of these examples?

1. Hum in your head

This WORKS. Best in situations where you feel like people are watching you and don't know where to look.

2. Pretend you already know them

Most people will be either too polite or too worried they actually did meet you and have forgotten to correct you, meaning they will be compelled to talk to you anyway.

3. Smile confidently

Can trick both others and yourself into thinking you are confident and relaxed in the situation. Likely to draw any other similarly lost/awkward people towards you, thereby solving both your problems.

4. Remember everyone else probably feels the same way

Scientifically, 89 per cent of the time that you're mortified that everyone is staring at you thinking how weird you are, they are actually busy being mortified that everyone is staring at them thinking how weird they are. Fact.

5. Tell a joke

If it's funny, people will immediately like you and talk to you. If it's not funny, people will either talk to you out of sympathy or feel a bit better about themselves, which will make them like you more. Win win. No fart jokes!

6. Look for the person who looks like you feel

Find somebody who is feeling just as nervous or awkward as you are and you'll both be so relieved to have someone to talk to you'll get on like a house on fire. This works particularly well on first days at a new school/university/ summer camp, when everybody is in the same boat.

WAYS NOT TO DEAL WITH UNCOMFORTABLE MOMENTS WHEN YOU FEEL UNPOPULAR OR AWKWARD

1 Do an ironic wave

Rarely comes off the cool way you intended, ends up making you look really, really weird. (Happened to a friend.)

2 Leave the room

So tempting but makes things even worse when you inevitably have to come back in again as you needed to be there in the first place.

3 Make a pretend phone call

Someone may actually ring you while you are doing it, so the phone starts going off while you're holding it to your ear fake-talking into it. (That was a bad day.)

The thing about those awkward and humiliating moments is that literally *everybody* has them. There is nobody in the history of the world who has just rocked up and found themselves the coolest kid in the class. And when you're in the middle of one of those moments, it seems 100 times worse to you than it does to the casual observer, I *promise*. In fact, a lot of those terrifying teenage moments that we see emblazoned across our screens are actually a lot less scary in real life. Contrary to what *Gossip Girl* and others might have you believe, there is no literal popularity police, total social decimation doesn't necessarily follow a chipped nail, mis-matched accessories aren't going to lead to social suicide, and not everybody's a bitch or a mean girl.

In fact, I'm not sure 'bitches' and 'mean girls' exist at all . . .

I'm not saying girls can't be mean. I'm just not sure the reason they're mean is because they're girls, or that girls are biologically pre-programmed to hate other girls. In fact, I'm sure they're not.

Of course I know there can be mean girls, as in girls who are mean, just like there are mean guys and mean people generally. But the bubble-gum popping, lip-gloss wearing, pink mini-skirted ice princess with her posse of dumb, thin friends who are just as bitchy but with slightly smaller boobs? It's a hollow stereotype.

Just like it's way too simple to blame the under-representation of women in top jobs on women themselves, it's also too easy to suggest that teenage girls sometimes have a tough time because there are witchy, bitchy she-devils in their midst.

And the mean girl isn't the only stereotype that's projected onto teenage girls, there's a whole cast of other equally unrealistic characters:

The Girly Girl

She prefers feathers, fluff, glitter and gloss, and won't be caught dead in a hoodie. Everything matches. Everything is pink. Sport is 'ew', shopping is 'yay'. Yawn.

The Bimbo

She's blonde, naturally (but probably not naturally). She's dumb, but she has big boobs so some guy does her homework for her. Superpower: twirling her hair around her finger.

The Tomboy

She would rather shit in her hands and clap than be caught in a dress and she's permanently up a tree. She's not interested in boys and she hates underwear. She's probably close to her dad, because how else does a girl get into sports?

The Geek Girl

She's obsessed with computer games and *The Big Bang Theory*. She wears thick-rimmed glasses and her hair is sometimes blue. She wears a Rubik's cube necklace, only laughs at inside jokes and probably runs the Anonymous Twitter account. Her only friends are on online forums.

The Fat Girl

She's always eating, never active, and doesn't have any friends. She dresses unfashionably and is ashamed of being fat. No guy would ever talk to her. She's always the butt of jokes, never the one making them.

The Prude

She's uptight and shy, wears her blouses buttoned to the neck and has never kissed a guy. She has over-protective parents and she's either too 'swotty' or too religious to be interested in boys.

The Mouthy Feminist

She's always banging on about women's rights, she wears dungarees, never shaves her armpits and is probably a lesbian, which is obviously an insult. She probably just needs a good shag to loosen her up, amirite?

All of this would be fine, if any of these people had ever actually existed in real life. And if it weren't ridiculously offensive, obviously. Maybe the blonde is actually really fucking good at chess, maybe the mouthy feminist is painfully shy and maybe the girl up a tree actually climbed it because she fancies the pants off someone next door. Last time I checked, hair colour had zero to do with intelligence and glitter eyeshadow wasn't an 'all the time or never' kind of deal. Being bigger doesn't mean someone is lazy or greedy and it doesn't have any impact on how funny they are. Liking comics doesn't mean you don't know how to talk about anything else and being a feminist doesn't mean you hate men. And this might come as a huge shock to Hollywood but a girl can get along just fine without a date and STILL have other character traits, interests and hobbies. It's almost like our lives don't completely revolve around guys!

You might be all of these girls, you might be none of these girls, you might relate to one or two but the point is you are an individual and you should never confine yourself to a box assigned to you by society.

Don't buy into the myth. Don't put other girls down, or perpetuate stereotypes. If someone is mean, it's more than likely there's a sad reason. Framing them with a stupid stereotype doesn't help. In fact, the most powerful, intelligent, brave thing you can do is to offer other girls your friendship. Don't let stereotypes turn you against one another. Reach out and stand up for each other. We've all heard the nonsense: blondes have more fun, redheads are firebrands, guys don't make passes at girls who wear glasses and diamonds are a girl's best friend. Vomit.

Don't fall for it. Be a revolutionary. Support other girls and let them support you. You'll be creating your own strongest support team *and* subverting social norms all in one fell swoop. Or, as my wonderful friend Jo (who just happened to illustrate this book) likes to put it . . .

And while you're at it, here's another stereotype you can bust wide open: the quiet, tortured young woman who bottles up her emotions and doesn't talk to anybody. Seriously not all it's cracked up to be. One of the phrases girls say most often is this:

'I'm fine.'

Even when you're not.

Why? Talking things through makes you feel better 99.9 per cent of the time. Even if it doesn't solve the problem, it can help you think more clearly and feel supported. Being the strong, silent type isn't worth it. If you're always there for your friends, then sometimes you have to let your friends be there for you.

Life advice is all well and good (especially if it tells you to trust your gut, because mine is usually saying 'cake'). But sometimes it takes more than a motivational poster or even a good friend to make you feel better. Sometimes you can't seem to feel better, no matter how hard you try. If you're feeling persistently low, or so intensely upset or anxious that you feel like you can't handle your emotions, it's possible that you might be experiencing depression, anxiety or some form of mental health problem.

The phrase 'mental health' can sound scary, but it's mostly because of society's stereotypes. Having a period of poor mental health is really common – in fact, according to the charity Mind, one in four people in the UK will each year.

Some signs include:

- Feeling constantly angry, annoyed or upset
- Feeling like there's no point in anything and it's difficult to keep going
- Having trouble sleeping or sleeping too much
- Finding it difficult to concentrate

- Taking no pleasure in activities you used to enjoy
- Feeling bad about yourself, or like you are worthless
- Thinking about death or suicide

If you are finding yourself thinking about death or suicide, please put this book down and go and talk to someone about it right now. You can do it. People are there for you and they want to help. It doesn't matter whether it's a parent, a friend, a GP or the Papyrus helpline for suicidal young people (0800 068 41 41) – just reach out and you will find that support is right there waiting for you.

There's a lot of silly stigma about mental health, but contrary to popular myths, mental health issues aren't contagious, they don't necessarily last forever, and they don't make you dangerous. It doesn't mean there's anything 'wrong' or 'weird' about you – depression and anxiety aren't part of you. They're not part of your personality. They're illnesses, like having a sore throat or a broken leg.

It's also not something you can just 'snap out of' or 'shake off', so telling someone to just cheer up is not helpful. In fact, it's about as helpful as telling someone with a black eye to just wipe it off, or shoving someone out of a wheelchair and saying they'll be able to walk if they just 'think positive'.

Eating disorders are another common mental health problem and can affect people of all genders, ages and backgrounds. There's no single cause and not everyone will experience the same symptoms, but signs might include an obsession with controlling body weight or food intake; fear of fatness; making excuses not to eat; excessive calorie counting; missing meals; excessive exercise; taking diet pills; vomiting or misusing laxatives (purging). They might also include eating large amounts of food very quickly; eating when not hungry; eating until you're uncomfortably full;

feeling guilt, shame or powerlessness about eating; and being preoccupied with thoughts about food.

It's OK to be clear and adamant that there's a problem if someone is trying to tell you it's not a big deal. It is a big deal. I'm saying this because I've heard from a lot of teenage girls who've experienced mental health problems and heard things like, 'What's a pretty girl like you got to worry about?' or 'Maybe you just need a shopping trip to perk you up.' Don't be fobbed off – you deserve support and it's available for you, so don't take no for an answer. Don't feel like it's 'too minor' or you 'shouldn't bother' anyone – help is there for you and you deserve it. Even if you're not sure if you have any of the symptoms I've discussed, if you're worried and upset by something, it's important to talk it through. Your feelings matter.

You might also recognize some of the above symptoms in a friend, in which case it's important to be there to support them too. You can encourage them to talk about how they are feeling, and support them by listening and spending time with them. You could help them book a doctor's appointment, or go with them, or help them look up resources online (more at the back of the book).

Another thing that depression and struggling with emotions can be linked to is self-harm, which means deliberately hurting yourself, sometimes by cutting, burning, scratching or hair pulling. This is often interpreted as a 'cry for help' or an attempt at suicide, but more often it is a way of trying to feel in control – perhaps using physical pain as a way to avoid dealing with emotional pain.

According to ChildLine, these are the top things that young people have reported finding helpful when dealing with self-harm:

- Listening to music
- Talking to friends or family
- Writing down how you feel
- Drawing a butterfly on yourself – the aim is to keep it alive and if you self-harm you 'kill' the butterfly
- Exercise
- Squeezing an ice cube

They also recommend trying to focus on the emotion that makes you feel like self-harming, and thinking about other ways to try and cope with that feeling – like going for a run, punching a pillow or screaming if it's anger; organizing, cleaning something or doing a puzzle if it's feeling out of control; writing, painting or listing good things about yourself if it's low self-esteem.

One of the top things recommended to help with mental health problems is exercise, because our physical and mental health are closely linked. When you exercise, your brain releases endorphins (sometimes known as 'feelgood' hormones), which can calm anxiety and lift your mood. It can also help you to reduce stress and tension and to feel more in control. AND it can give your self-esteem a big boost. What's not to love? (If you just answered: 'running!', I feel you – but remember that swimming, walking, tobogganing, shopping and ringing the doorbell then running away are all technically types of exercise too.)

It's no surprise that young people sometimes struggle with mental health. You know how I mentioned that young women are basically the strongest people in the world? Well, they deal with all that other stuff *on top of* taking gruelling exams that could have a major impact on their future and probably working harder and learning more than they ever will at any other time in their lives. It's exhausting just thinking about it. All that pressure can cause a lot of stress, and this is as good a time as any to learn some ways to cope with it, because life inevitably has its ups and downs and stress is something that we all have to deal with every now and then.

Nobody can give you a magic pill to take away your stress entirely, because what works for some people won't work for others, and you need to experiment yourself to find out if you're the person who finds a brisk walk helpful to take their mind off something, or the person who uses a long, hot bath to help themselves feel better. But here's a good rule of thumb:

IF IT MAKES YOU FEEL GOOD, KEEP DOING IT.
IF IT MAKES YOU FEEL BAD, STOP.

This rule is immensely useful. It works for everything from relationships to friendships to magazines to make-up to dieting. OK, it doesn't work for *absolutely* everything (exams, for example). But it's generally pretty effective.

It sounds so obvious, because we assume that anybody would stop doing anything that made them feel bad. But actually, that's not the case at all. Think of the number of things we keep doing in our lives even though they make us feel bad. Like hanging out with friends who aren't supportive, because we feel like we have a duty to them, or we're worried we'll be a loner if we don't stick with them. Worrying about our bodies and faces because women's magazines tell us to. Staying in unsupportive relationships because we're scared of breaking up. Eating spinach.

Some of these things we can't change (you kind of need to eat your greens). But some of them we can: by choosing to put ourselves and our happiness first. It's not easy – if it was, we'd all be doing it already. But it's something we can practise and work on, and hopefully get better at over time.

The good news is that there are some things that make us feel good that are actually really easy to do more of. They might include talking to friends, spending time outdoors, curling up with a great book, having a cup of tea, writing a diary, playing computer games, painting, sitting in the sunshine, having a picnic, or anything else that makes you feel calm and relaxed. It's very important to remember to do a little something like this each day, even when you're particularly stressed, or in the middle of exams.

Whether you're worrying about essays, relationships or popularity, it's really important to take a moment every now and then to look after yourself and get your balance back.

And if you are feeling worried about any of those things, if you're feeling small, or unpopular, rejected or unimportant, just remember …

You never know what's going to happen tomorrow.

In my early twenties, I moved to London to try to be an actress, which means that my advice about rejection, humiliation and failure comes from the best possible place – my own repeated and painful experience.

The glamorous world of acting was nothing I thought it would be and less. I bounced from audition to audition looking for my big acting break. I read for the role of Daenerys Targaryen in *Game of Thrones* in a dingy, airless room underneath a church in central London and was sent out of the room practically before I'd opened my mouth.

I was sent away time and again feeling like a failure. But from one of those auditions I also learned a valuable lesson about those situations where you feel like the smallest person in the world. I turned up one morning at a huge London TV studio to audition for a new major series that required a combination of actors, musicians and dancers. (I was hoping you didn't have to be great at all three. OK, I was hoping you only needed to be able to do one. Semi-well.)

We were paired up for the auditions, in boy-girl pairs, and my partner, a scruffy, sweet-faced boy clutching his guitar for dear life, was even more nervous than I was, which made me feel the tiniest bit better.

Ushered into the audition room in front of two stony-faced executives, we stumbled our way through a few pages of dialogue and found ourselves back outside without much hope that we'd done anything at all to recommend ourselves. Everybody in the building, from the kind but brusque execs to the person who swept us out of the door, made it very clear that we were tiny, unimportant minnows in a very, very big pond.

As we walked out of the building, he looked down and realized his demo CD was still clutched in his slightly trembling hand – he'd been so nervous he'd completely forgotten to hand it to the producers. Rather forlornly, he offered it to me instead. I felt sorry for him, so I took it home to be polite, then tossed it in the back of a drawer and never listened to it.

Needless to say, neither of us got the part. But just a few years later that scruffy kid who trembled alongside me while we were made to feel like the smallest people in the world is kind of a big deal. His name is Ed Sheeran.

A lot of the time people tell that kind of story about how you never know what's going to happen as a kind of parable to explain that you should always treat other people nicely because you never know who they might eventually be. I think that's quite flawed – you should be nice to everybody regardless of their potential future career. But I do think it's a useful story to look at the other way around. When the people around you make you feel small and ridiculous and awkward, it's worth remembering that this is just a moment of your journey on your way somewhere else. Neither you nor they have any idea yet where you're going to end up and just how stupid they might later feel for treating you that way. (Or throwing away your CD. Sorry, Ed.)

CHAPTER FIVE

THAT'S NOT YOUR VAGINA

We need to talk about genitals. We need to talk about hoohas and doodahs and winkies and twinkies and we need to talk about why we can't use the real names when we discuss them. We need to ask why we've tried so desperately to avoid talking frankly about genitalia that we've managed to come up with an impressively long list of alternative words to describe them. Trust me – I've Googled them so you don't have to. (And yes, I had to answer some pretty awkward questions about my search history. You're welcome.)

We can't manage 'vagina' or 'vulva' but we'll happily say:

Chach

Choot

Chocha

Clunge

Cock socket

Cherry

Chonch

Fanny

Hatchet wound (:/)

Flange

Taco

Cat flaps

Front bottom

Cha Cha

Chuff

Hoo hoo

Kitty

Grumble

Furburger (for some reason this irresistibly makes me think of a Muppet but I can't exactly put my finger on why)

Love cave

Hooch

Minge

Muff

Camel toe

Beef curtains

Pookie

Box

Pootang

Poontang

Clam

Pootie

Cooter

Quiff

Beaver

Piss flaps

Hooha

Love tunnel

Cunt

Vadge

Vajizzle

Slit

Wizard sleeve

Bearded Oyster

Woohoo

Snatch

Quim

Sheath

Poonany

Twat

Bang hole

Artichoke

Coochie

Oyster

Poon

Bank

Bat cave

Vajayjay

Pussy

Bearded Clam

Twinkle Cave

Axe wound (:/)

Sashimi (and if that doesn't put you off sushi I don't know what will)

Auntie Jean

We cringe from saying 'penis' but we don't mind talking about a:

Shaft

Sword

Beaver cleaver

Helmet

Love muscle

Love shaft

Jack-in-the-box

Love stick

Main vein

Baby arm

Manhood

Bobby dangler

Bratwurst

Chub

Chopper

Dangler

Chap

The D

D train

Ding-a-ling

Ding

Hotdog

Domepiece

Man muscle

Joystick

Jimmy

Patz

Knob

Peen

Lady boner

Member

Winkie

Third leg

Pee-pee

Pecker

Peepster

Wood

Peter

Willy

Arrow

PhD

Anaconda

Baloney

Pickle

Pole   Beef bayonet

Piece

Pocket rocket

Rod   Choad (try not to be distracted by the
             fact that this is the funniest word you

Bishop   will ever see written down. I understand
             that you may need a moment.)

Salami

Tripod   Unit

Purple-headed warrior   Wang

Dick   Cock

Sausage

Dong

Dork

Schmeckel

Skin flute

Hose

Tent pole   Meat

Johnson   Knob

Throbber

John Thomas   Pecker

Tonsil tickler

Pipe   Wiener

Peter

Tool

Prick   Schlong   (One-eyed)
                                 trouser snake

For the record, I have looked it up and the much-disputed plural of
penis is sadly not penii, which is somehow just a joyfully hilarious
word. I'm afraid it is actually 'penises', which sounds much more

sensible. But if it makes you feel any better you can also officially use 'penes', which is satisfyingly sniggerworthy. I haven't been able to authoritatively discover what the collective noun (like a *school* of fish or *flock* of sheep) is for penises, but suggestions on my Facebook page included a cluster, a bulge, a knot, which just sounds painful, or a bouquet. Which is a delightful image.

Let me give you a moment to think about that.

＊

You might notice that the words for women's genitalia are sometimes derogatory or violent (like 'gash' or 'axe wound'). Often they suggest the vagina is just there as a receptacle for a man's penis (like 'sheath' or 'cock socket').

It's important to talk about bodies, and about genitals, because they're things that we don't often get the chance to discuss. And because even when we do, we're often given bad information. A lot of this bad information, particularly relating to women's genitalia, can be found online.

The other day I saw an image on a social media feed that showed photographs of two different vulvas: one with quite visible labia and one that looked Photoshopped and smooth as a Barbie's bottom. The caption on the second image read: 'Non-whore pussy (low mileage)' and on the first: 'Whore pussy (many miles of cock)'.

This is absolute nonsense. Nonsense, I tell you! People's genitals come in all different shapes, sizes, colours and styles. The way they look has no bearing on how good they feel to have sex with (spoiler alert: all genitals can feel pretty great to have sex with). And you absolutely can't tell how much sex someone has had by looking at their bits. It just doesn't work like that. It's completely normal for women's labia to be different sizes on different sides too. Sex doesn't stretch out or 'loosen' a vagina, or make the labia ('lips' – diagram coming up) longer or more protruding, any more than regular masturbation shrinks a guy's penis. These are urban legends and when you think about it, they're kinda ridiculous. How many porn stars do you know whose penises have disappeared from having so much sex? Sadly, a lot of these myths revolve around the idea that a woman's genitals should look as doll-like and young and frankly weirdly plastic as possible. A lot of the external female genitalia we see online and in porn have been shaved and even altered with plastic surgery to make them look more uniform and apparently 'attractive'. The fashion for getting rid of all pubic hair is in large part driven by the porn industry, and arises from a desire for viewers to see penetration as clearly as possible. But the reality is that we are all different. There are all kinds of different vulvas, labia, and clitorises. And all genitals are good genitals. They're also very friendly – get to know yours today, they won't bite!

Some people like to give their body bits their own more personal names, like calling your penis your tin soldier, or Mr Mustachio, or Little Pete. Some people like to give their breasts names, like the Fantastits, or Ant and Dec, or Colonel and the Professor. There's nothing wrong with naming your own body parts, especially if it makes it easier to talk about them. Sometimes communicating with your partner about body bits can be easier with a bit of laughter – that's fine! But you should never be made to feel ashamed or dirty for using the scientific terms for your body parts either.

is NOT a
dirty word*

*NEITHER IS VULVA, LABIA, CLITORIS OR CERVIX

It really isn't. Vagina vagina vagina vagina vagina. VAGINA.
VAAAGGGIIINNNNAAAAAAAAA.

VAG

INA

Ahem.

We need to talk about vaginas. We need to talk about why it's easier to say penis than to say vagina. (Don't believe me? Apple will let you engrave the word 'penis' on your iPhone, but not the word 'vagina'. Go ahead, Google it.) Apple really needs to girl up. My predictive text is so freaked out about me using the word 'vagina' it will literally suggest pretty much *any* alternative words. Things it has recently changed 'vagina' to include: 'basic', 'bahia casks', and 'bernina', which I'm pretty sure is not even a real thing. Rude.

(Then again, it also keeps changing penis to 'penistone', which sounds awesome and I want one, so at least it is equal opportunities prudery.)

We need to talk about how we're so confused about genitals that we use the word 'vagina' when we really mean vulva. We need to talk about body parts and what they look like and how they work, because when we know more about our own bodies we are much more powerful and in control over how they are used. And we should all know about all the genitalia, not just our own – because it makes us more comfortable and confident if we want to have sex, because it increases our ability to pleasure our partner and to tell them exactly how to pleasure us, and because you never know when you might be stuck in the lift with someone who has a bona fide genital emergency and how bad would you feel if you weren't equipped to help out?

Generally speaking, female anatomy gets a particularly raw deal. (Somehow that sentence sounds sore and I apologize for writing it down.) There have actually been biology text books where the clitoris isn't even included in the diagram, because someone in their great wisdom decided girls might get funny ideas about pleasure and didn't need to know about the Single. Most. Awesome. Organ. Ever. Hell, were they wrong!

We all have a fairly clear idea of what a penis and testicles look like (school graffiti artists nationwide, I salute you) but the lack of general knowledge about vulvas, vaginas, labia and clitorises (clitori? cliterati?) is quite surprising. I discovered this in my second year at university, when I was sitting in the dining hall having dinner one night with a group of the most intelligent guys I'd ever met. I don't remember how the conversation came around to it (honestly), but somehow we started discussing female genitalia. And you know what? Out of maybe nineteen or twenty guys (it was a long table), it turned out that all but a handful of them thought women HAD TWO HOLES. That's right. The vast majority of my highly educated male university peers thought women pooped out of one hole and both sexed and peed through the other. It was pretty weird. These were not guys who hadn't had hands-on experience either, if you know what I mean. Just as I was reeling from this, several of the women present looked at me blankly and asked what the problem was, because they thought that was how it worked too. Then, just as I was laughing my head off at them, and explaining that there are actually three holes, somebody else pointed out to *me* that you don't actually pee through your clitoris and I, too, was stumped. I had always thought the urethral opening came out through the middle of the little bump that is the clitoris. Yes, I know that's ridiculous. No, your clitoris doesn't have a hole in it. Well, I know that *now*.

As we've already established, your vagina is not necessarily what makes you a girl or a woman. But for those folk that have one, it is worth knowing a bit more about your bits and pieces. And for those who don't, you never know when this info might come in handy. For those of us who don't have the benefit of the *infinite* wisdom of Sophia from *Orange Is the New Black* (*bow down*), here's the deal:

ANATOMY
of the
Vulva

COLOUR by
NUMBERS *

1. LIME GREEN
2. BRIGHT ORANGE
3. TURQUOISE
4. HOT PINK
5. LILAC

LABIA MAJORA

LABIA MINORA

CLITORA HOOD

VAGINAL ENTRANCE

PERINEUM

ANUS

1.

2.

3.

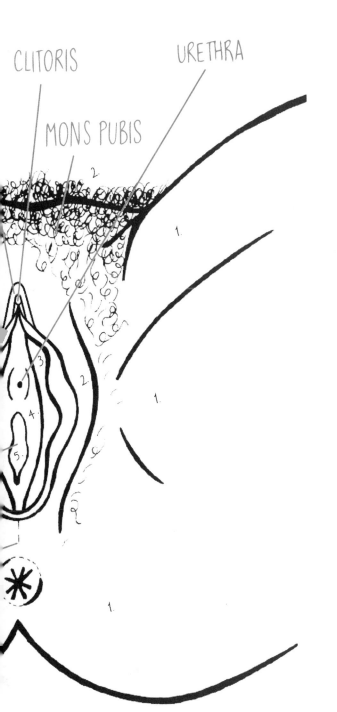

CLITORIS

URETHRA

MONS PUBIS

2.

1.

3.

2.

4.

1.

5.

1.

* COLOURS MAY
BE UNREALISTIC
DUE TO EVERYONE'S
UNIQUENESS

Some important stuff about this:

- THAT'S NOT YOUR VAGINA! The word 'vulva' describes all the parts of your genitals that you can see outside the body, including the mons pubis (Latin for 'pubic mound'), labia majora (outer lips), labia minora (inner lips), clitoris, and the external openings of the urethra and vagina. The only part of your vagina that you can see from the outside is the opening, yet in popular culture people often say 'vagina' when they mean 'vulva'. Look out for this, because there are many ripe opportunities to cry: 'THAT'S NOT YOUR VAGINA!', which is a delightful thing to do in public and so pleasurable that it was almost the title of this book.

- All the bits and pieces might be a different size/shape/ colour for different people, which is 100 per cent normal. (Unless they're lime green or electric blue, in which case you may in fact be some kind of parrot.) If you're at all worried about anything, you can always ask your GP to check it over to put your mind at rest.

- It is completely normal to have pubic hair not only covering your mons pubis but also around your vulva and anus. Some people choose to shave or wax some of this hair, others like to just trim the edges, and others leave it completely natural. The choice is yours and yours alone. Waxing and shaving are generally quite new practices, driven by the appearance of women's genitals in the porn industry. Nobody who has sex with you should get to choose what happens to your pubic hair any more than you have the right to tell them what to do with theirs. It's worth bearing in mind that pubic hair is intended to prevent friction and does a pretty great job of it too! And if you shave or wax it off you can experience some itchy prickliness while it grows back. #JustSayin

- Touching or pressing on the mons pubis (also sometimes known as the mound of venus) can be pleasurable, because it has lots of nerve-endings and can indirectly stimulate the clitoris.

Although it's great to know about these parts of your body, remember that the genitals are not the only area involved in sex. Other areas of the body contain hundreds of sensitive nerve-endings and touching, stroking, licking and kissing them can be a huge turn-on, including: lips and mouth, ears, neck, shoulders, breasts, nipples, stomach, inner thighs and toes (for some people – you'll be able to tell who they are because they'll be the ones writhing in pleasure instead of giggling hysterically).

Which bits respond to the touch and turn you on will vary from person to person and even from day to day. It's not about which gender you identify as either – where you like to be touched is unique to you.

THINGS YOU DIDN'T KNOW ABOUT YOUR CLITORIS

1. Your clitoris is the only organ in the whole body solely devoted to pleasure – win! It contains around 8,000 nerve-endings and it can be incredibly sensitive during arousal. Some people find direct stimulation intensely

erotic, others prefer it to be stimulated more gently, through the clitoral hood, or the surrounding areas. It can be stimulated through touching, rubbing, licking, kissing and sucking.

2. If you're struggling to locate it, explore with your fingers by feeling your way up the outer labia from the bottom (or back side) to the top (or front side) where they join – the clitoris is located there at the top.

3. The clitoris also stiffens and becomes slightly larger during sex, just like the penis. When you are aroused it should be easier to find because it should be particularly sensitive to the touch. Using a small vibrator to feel around your labia is another good way to find it – when you bring the vibrator nearer to the clitoris it should feel particularly arousing for most people. If you're still struggling to find it, ask your gynaecologist or GP to show you where it is; it's absolutely fine to ask.

4. People who have some form of paralysis or nerve disruption can still often experience different degrees of sensation and stimulation. Just like with anybody else, the best way to discover is to explore, with or without a partner.

5. You don't wee through it! The urethral opening is located close to the clitoris so it's not an uncommon misconception to think that that is where the wee is coming from.

6. Because so much of the clitoris is internal, it can be stimulated from the inside as well, through vaginal sex. This also means that your clitoris is part of the

orgasm from different places as it sort of hugs your vagina (ahhh) so the idea of having *either* a 'clitoral' *or* a 'vaginal' orgasm, which you might have heard of, is actually kind of misleading. The fact that so much of the clitoris is inside the body also means that people who have experienced some form of clitoral mutilation may also experience clitoral sensation as some of the clitoris remains.

Just like the labia, the size and shape of the clitoris varies from person to person.

Pop Quiz: What do your clitoris and the iceberg that sank the *Titanic* have in common? Answer: They're both waaaay bigger and more impactful that you might think. They can both trigger earth-shattering events. But you can only see the tip of each one. Most of the clitoris is inside your body – in fact, check it out overleaf in all its magnificent glory, alongside some regular household objects so you can see just how big it is . . .

THE CLITORIS

GLANS CLITORIS

URETHRAL OPENIN

VAGINAL OPENIN

CORPUS CAVERNOSUM

CRUS CLITORIS

BULB OF VESTIBULE

DID YOU KNOW?

THE AVERAGE CLITORIS IS 3.5" TO 5" LONG AND 2.5" WIDE

Now in case they're feeling left out, here's some vital info about willies (an encyclopenia, if you will).

- Some are longer than others but the average adult penis size is smaller than you might think (or lads' chat might have you believe) at about 14–16cm when erect, according to the NHS. These figures were calculated by measuring 11,531 penises, or, as one poor person might remember it, the Longest. Summer. Job. Ever.

- Contrary to a great deal of unnecessary but understand-able angst, penis size doesn't have a lot to do with sexual performance. The sensitive nerve-endings inside the vagina are concentrated towards the entrance and the first inch or two, so much length beyond this is largely irrelevant to sensation.

- Penises get erect when men are aroused and blood rushes into the penile tissue, causing it to stiffen and start to point outwards and upwards. This can happen at inopportune moments, which can be pretty embarrassing, especially during teenage years, and can lead to the classic 'tucking it under your belt' manoeuvre. It can be completely non-sexual, and doesn't necessarily mean he is turned on by that calculus problem/airport scanner/supermarket checkout.

- Their 'resting' length has little correlation to the length when ready for action – the old 'grower' or 'shower' saying is actually quite accurate.

- Some are circumcised, which means the foreskin has been removed, others are uncircumcised, which means the foreskin remains intact but it naturally slides back from the head of the penis when it is erect. (If the foreskin is very tight, or won't slide back, it might be worth checking it out with a doctor.)

- Circumcised or not it doesn't make a lot of difference, but either way, HYGIENE IS KEY. As the saying goes, 'nobody likes a stinky penis'. Actually it's not really a 'saying' so much as a helpful rule for life – like: 'nobody likes a penis at the dinner table' or 'never put your penis in the fire'. Say it with me: nobody likes a stinky penis. In fact, whenever women are surveyed about penises, the results almost always show that they care more about cleanliness than ANY other aspect, including size. There is no such thing as a 'penis smell' – penises don't smell of anything – but there is such a thing as a 'dirty penis smell' – it smells like old sweat, dry urine and lack of consideration, with a slight tang of cheesiness you can't quite put your finger on. You have been warned.

- Some curve slightly. This is what the tailoring term 'dress to the left' or 'dress to the right' means. It's a polite way of saying, 'Which side of your trousers should I allow a little extra space on so your willy can hang down the leg ... Sir?'

- The prostate gland can be found inside the rectum and stimulation can be very pleasurable for people who have one (people who have penises also have a prostate gland).

- One both wees and ejaculates through the penis, but, luckily for everyone involved, not at the same time. This is another reason why good hygiene is key for an enjoyable and healthy sex life.

Getting to know your body doesn't have to start with someone else. It's a good idea to know lots about our bodies – knowing what our moles look like and where they are can help us spot any early signs of skin cancer, for example, and knowing how our breasts or testicles feel can help us notice if they change.

It can also help to explore your own body in a more sexual way, for lots of reasons. Firstly, it can feel bloody brilliant. Secondly, it can help you to get to know yourself, your likes and dislikes, your preferences and sensitivities. Knowing this stuff makes it much easier to pass the info on to a sexual partner later on. And trust me, you want your sexual partner to have as much info about what turns you on as possible. (If exploring your own body isn't something you feel you want to do at this stage, that's also perfectly fine – there's no pressure and it definitely isn't a race. Your genitals aren't going anywhere, they'll be ready whenever you are.)

So how do you get to know your body? Lots of people advise using a hand mirror to explore your genitals, which is odd, because in my experience only Disney princesses own hand mirrors. (And we all know they don't have any genitalia.) You can easily use a make-up compact mirror though, unless you're a talented enough gymnast to use a standing mirror. I tried that and ended up flat on my face with my ankle wrapped around my neck – neither sexy nor comfortable. Then I came up with the novel idea of lying the mirror flat on the floor and squatting. Awesome plan until your dad walks in – this scenario is *greatly* improved by a lockable door.

But exploring through touch and feel is just as important as looking. Make sure you have clean hands, and preferably short nails (more wisdom learned by painful experience). Some people find it easiest to do this in the bath. Others feel most comfortable lying in bed, or sitting on the toilet. Using a lubricant (which you can buy in most pharmacies) might help. Be gentle, take your time, and let yourself explore what feels good. There is no right or wrong, just what feels good to you.

If you have a vagina you can also try to work out where your G-spot might be, though bear in mind there is a lot of debate about whether it even exists or whether everybody has one. The G-spot is thought to be a sort of spongy, gently ridged patch about the size of a small coin, located on the belly button-side inside wall of your vagina. It's about an inch and a half from the vaginal opening, so you might be able to explore it with a middle fingertip.

Some people find G-spot or more general vaginal stimulation pleasurable, and many enjoy clitoral stimulation. Some like light pressure or stroking around the anus, or the area between the vagina and anus (called the perineum). Bear in mind that if you touch or insert a finger in your anus you want to wash that finger before touching your vagina with it in case of cross-infection, just because the anus tends to have more poo-related germs around. For lots of people, touching a combination of places is the jackpot. (This led to the legendary and gloriously named 'Venus butterfly' technique, which involves stimulating clitoris, vagina and perineum/anus simultaneously!) Some like it harder and faster, others softer and gentler. Or both! You won't know till you try.

If you have a penis, you can experiment with touching, stroking and rubbing the shaft, testicles, perineum and anus as well as other areas of your body. (Did you know nipple stimulation can be super pleasurable for people of any gender, not just women?)

Our culture has a long and embarrassing history of making people feel dirty or ashamed about masturbation. We portray it as some-thing sinful that people should keep hidden. But it's actually pretty responsible. We wouldn't go into any other major life experience without practising first, so what's so different about sex? Think of it like driving practice, except without the L-plates and the instructor

MASTUR
IS

BATION

NORMAL

(both of which would be pretty weird in this situation). It's also a good way to satisfy your own sexual desires if you are under the age of consent or don't happen to have an enthusiastic partner to practise with!

The great thing about solo exploring and masturbation is that there's no risk involved. You're not risking an STI. There's no risk of pregnancy. You won't leave any tell-tale signs of what you've been doing if you don't want anybody to know. As already discussed, you won't change your body, or make your vagina 'looser' by masturbating. And contrary to an ancient and ridiculous myth, you DEFINITELY won't go blind.

In fact, far from being something shameful, it's actually a time-honoured tradition. People have been doing it for centuries. Abraham Lincoln probably did it. Jane Austen. Father Christmas. You just *know* someone's tried it in space and then had to scramble around trying to get all the little floating globules cleaned up before the other astronauts came over from the International Space Station.

You can also explore using a vibrator (vibrating toys of different shapes and sizes, usually used to stimulate the external genitals and clitoris) or a dildo (shaped like a penis, doesn't usually vibrate), or even just by using a household object like a clean carrot (as long as you make sure to cover it with a condom first and throw it away afterwards). Avoid anything sharp or pointy, or anything that could splinter or break off. Also, pro-tip: if you're using a vegetable of any kind, don't take one from right at the back of the fridge, in case it's frozen. Don't ask me how I know. Just trust me on this one.

If you're not able to get hold of a vibrator easily, there are household objects that vibrate which you might be able to use. They include electric toothbrushes (take off the bristled attachment and use the bottom end, covered with a condom), electric shavers (same deal – VERY important to take off the attachment and use the other end here), or even just regular vibrating massagers. But remember anything electric should never be used near water, always cover the item with a condom first, and only use items that belong to you – masturbating with someone else's toothbrush is a massive no-no. (Well, you wouldn't like it if they masturbated with yours, would you?)

✳

I didn't only call this chapter 'That's Not Your Vagina' because we so often mix up vulvas and vaginas when we talk about genitals. I also chose that title because it's something that sometimes needs to be said to other people. If you are the owner of a vagina (or any other body part for that matter) then nobody else has the right to do anything with it without your consent. And I mean nobody. Not a stranger. Not a friend. Not a family member. Not a sexual or romantic partner. Not somebody you've slept with before. Nobody gets to do anything you're not comfortable with. Nobody gets to touch you without your consent.

Sometimes it can be difficult to feel assertive about that, especially in a world that makes us feel like we have an obligation to be sexy all the time, or that we 'owe' sex to a partner, or that once we've had sex we are obliged to keep having it again. But not one of those things is true.

If ANYBODY pushes you into having any kind of sexual contact when you don't want to, it's sexual assault, no matter who, no matter what the circumstances.

If you're reading this and it's stirring up memories or difficult feelings, it's important to know that there is a huge amount of help and support available. You're never alone. There are details in the back of the book.

A question I get asked a lot when I visit schools is: is the victim of sexual assault ever to blame? Society repeatedly suggests to us that victims of rape and sexual offences are sometimes at least partly responsible for what happens. We see public figures talking about girls wearing short skirts and getting drunk and how unsafe it makes them. We watch internet forums tear rape victims apart because they had previously had sex with their rapist consensually, or they'd chosen to go to a hotel room with them, or they were drunk. We see police posters telling women to be careful, to watch their drinks, to stay in groups.

We get the message that women should be protecting themselves from rape – so is it their fault if they don't and they get raped?

The answer is no.

That doesn't really feel adequate.

The answer is:

Sorry, that doesn't really feel enough either. The answer is:

.

Hopefully that clears things up.

The thing is, we would never ask these questions about any other crime. If a person has their mobile phone stolen, we don't blame them for choosing to carry it, or walking down the wrong street at the wrong time. If somebody is a victim of fraud, we don't hear people asking if perhaps they were secretly enjoying it and only called it a crime afterwards. If somebody is robbed, we don't criticize them because 'they gave money away to charity in the past, so why shouldn't someone assume they could just take it?' The only person to blame is the perpetrator. Full stop.

Understanding that your body is yours alone and that you have the absolute right to decide who touches it, and how and when, is one of the strongest, most empowering things you will ever do.

Don't take it from me, take it from the bravest young woman I have ever met. She is kind, thoughtful, funny and clever and she asked for the following letter to be included in this book:

Dear Amazing Young Women,

I don't know you. I don't know what your interests or aspirations are, I don't know what's happened to you in your life, what your politics are, what you believe in, your regrets or what you are most proud of. I don't know who you love or why you love them. But I'm writing you this letter because I want the best for you and because I want to start a conversation with you that I wish someone had started with me ten years ago.

I want to talk about sex, relationships and consent. Because although it is so simple in so many ways, it is easily distorted, it can become confusing, and it can lead to painful and damaging situations. You may have heard a lot about sexual consent at school or through 'No Means No' campaigns, you may have seen stories about rape and domestic abuse in TV shows, you may have explored these ideas with your friends. But I wonder how much you have related this knowledge to your own experiences – perhaps when that guy at the party went just a little too far, or when your boyfriend wanted to sleep with you and you thought perhaps you should just do it. How did it make you feel?

Is it connected to these other images of rape and sexual violence? It may not feel like it.

I can only talk about my own experiences, but I believe it absolutely is. I have been raped, once by a friend after a night out and then quite a few times after that when I was in an abusive relationship. But the words 'rape' and 'abuse' are such strong words and so poorly understood that I was unable to name my experiences for over six years. These are things that happen to other people, really vulnerable people. Right? And anyway, surely if it happened to me it would be really obvious. Right?

Well, for me it wasn't at all obvious and that's what I'd like to talk to you about. It didn't feel how I'd expected rape to feel, it didn't look how I'd expected rape to look – I didn't scream, there was no physical restraint, no tears, no gruesome strangers in alleyways. It was simply me in a bedroom and people I'd trusted having sex with me after I'd said 'no'.

After these experiences I felt dirty, lonely, humiliated, embarrassed, ashamed and silenced. I felt as though I must be a freak and a prude. I felt it was my fault. I wanted to hide. Above all, I wanted to minimize it, I didn't want to talk about it or accept it, and I didn't for over half a decade. It's amazing the lengths my brain went to in order to deny my experiences, and ultimately how this denial kept me from moving forward and from being happy.

Self-blame and self-hatred were at the centre of it for me. I now know that in a weird way that was my brain trying to protect me. If I could make it my fault then I was the one in control and I could stop it from happening again and that would help me feel safe. But it also held me back and wore my self-esteem down so far that it became nearly impossible for me to sustain the relationships that followed.

I sincerely believe that if I had more knowledge about the realities of sex and sexual violence I would have been able to understand my experiences earlier, take better charge of them and stop them from having such a deep and long-term effect on my health and happiness.

There are some things I wish I'd known, lessons that have taken me years of pain and reflection to learn. I'd like to share them with you in the hope that they might help you in your journey. They are as follows:

– There is no 'normal' way to feel about sex or sexuality, everyone is different. I know someone who had sex for the first time when they were fourteen and another person when they were thirty-four and they both have equally healthy and fulfilling sex lives because they are doing what is right for them. People who judge others about their sexuality are either ignorant or extremely damaged themselves.

– You are not a freak and you don't have to conform to anyone else's expectations or standards.

– Rape, sexual violence and abuse rarely look like the stereotypical visions we are offered, and it's not always obvious when it happens to you.

– If you are having confusing emotions about any of your

sexual experiences, no matter how minor you think they might be, there are people who will listen, help you understand them and help you to move forwards (Rape Crisis etc.). No one on these lines will judge you or think you're exaggerating, overreacting or making it up (I understand how difficult this one is to believe, I have totally been there!).

– Always pay attention to your feelings and focus on exploring what feels right and healthy for you and your body. If it feels wrong to you, trust that feeling.

On top of this I wish I had learnt to love and esteem myself, I wish I had been able to trust myself and use that trust to gain deep knowledge of what felt nurturing and safe during sex and my relationships. But there is no instruction manual and no magic wand. I know you can't just switch on the self-love switch overnight, but trust me, it's worth working on. Catch yourself when you are being overly critical and ask yourself what you would be saying to a friend in the same situation – it's likely to be much kinder and more compassionate.

Above all I wish I'd known that I had the right to the exact type of sex life that felt right for me (so long as my partner was equally consenting, of course). You have that right, amazing young women; don't be afraid to live it.

All my love,

Your anonymous sister xx

CHAPTER SIX

DON'T BE SHY, AIM HIGH

During your life, people are probably going to tell you that you are and aren't good at things because of your sex. Under absolutely no circumstances should you listen to them.

Unfortunately, you probably shouldn't punch them either, as tempting as it may be.

The good news is that resisting the punchy urge will get easier with practice.

The bad news is you're going to get lots of practice.

If it helps, there is a vast amount of information available to help you shoot down ridiculous arguments . . .

They say: Girls aren't good at computers
You say: Yeah, apart from the fact that the first ever computer programmer, Ada Lovelace, was a woman. #Awkward

They say: Boys are just stronger than girls
You say: Mmmhmm, talk to me about Tomoe Gozen, the twelfth-

century samurai described as a 'warrior worth a thousand', or Marie Marvingt, the first female bomber pilot, or Harriet Tubman, who escaped from slavery and risked her own safety to rescue hundreds of others

They say: Politics is male-dominated because men are more natural leaders

You say: That's weird because Aung San Suu Kyi (the chairperson of the Burmese National League for Democracy, who won the Nobel Peace Prize for leading her people in peaceful protest against oppression), Angela Merkel (who has been the hugely successful Chancellor of Germany since 2005), Condoleezza Rice (the former US Secretary of State who pioneered the policy of Transformational Diplomacy to increase the number of responsible democratic governments internationally) and Ellen Johnson Sirleaf (who co-led a non-violent women's peace movement that helped bring an end to civil war and went on to become President of Liberia) WERE ALL WOMEN LAST TIME I CHECKED

They say: You're overreacting/being hysterical/on your period (delete as appropriate)

You say: *Or* I'm a woman voicing an opinion and that's freaking you out a little bit

They say: Wow, you're taking physics/engineering/other male-dominated subject – that's really unusual/tough for girls

You say: Lucky I've got role models like Marie Curie, the only person ever to win the Nobel Prize in both physics and chemistry, and the women who invented Kevlar, windscreen wipers and central heating. Oh and hey, do you like beer? Well, guess what? Women invented that too

They say: You don't *look* like a (insert male-dominated occupation or interest here)

You say: You don't *look* like a cockwomble. And yet . . .

They say: Your ambitions sound a bit high – let me tell you about the female-dominated career I think you would be better suited to

You say: Unfortunately I have approximately zero time to waste on your underestimation of my talent and potential – you feel free to keep chatting, but I'm going to have to go look up some job application information now

Truthfully, it's not always easy to be so bold. We hear things all the time that can make us question ourselves, doubt our abilities and think twice about putting ourselves forward, raising our hand, or aiming for the top. It's easy to feel like you're just pretending to know what you're doing, waiting all the time for someone to come and expose you. In fact, that feeling is so common it even has a name: imposter syndrome. But the truth is we all feel that way some of the time.

Generally speaking, guys are more comfortable faking it. This has absolutely zero to do with biology. As previously noted, we teach boys that it's cool and impressive and sexy for them to throw their weight around, act like they know what they're doing and generally swagger. We teach girls that it's cute and appealing for them to feign incompetence while asking for men's help.

(We also teach them if they pull this off really well and are very lucky God will send them a dude with a ukulele and a beard. I have no idea why this is an incentive.)

Anyway, the moral of the story is, girls, we need to learn to fake a little confidence too.

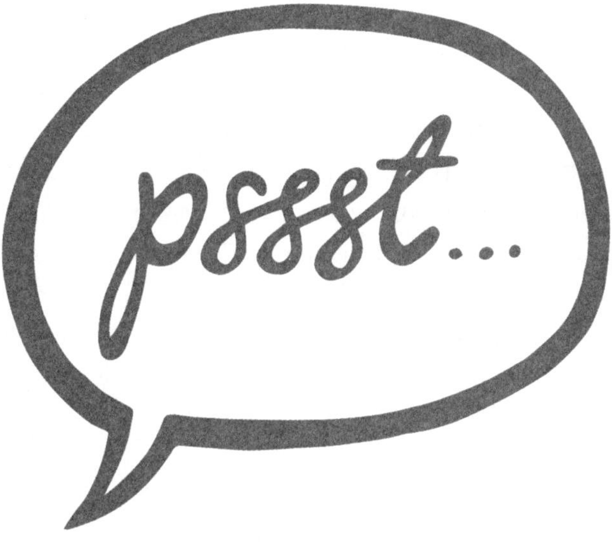
pssst...

...*nobody* has any IDEA what they are doing

I don't mean making things up. I don't mean pretending we have qualifications we don't. I just mean framing things more positively, and more assertively.

For example: take a look through your recent emails and text messages, and count up the number of times you used any of the following phrases:

- I just wondered
- Sorry
- So sorry
- Don't mean to
- If it'd be OK
- If you wouldn't mind
- Possibly
- Just
- Not at all
- Unless
- Totally fine
- If I could
- Apologies
- I'm afraid
- Unfortunately
- No problem
- No worries
- Totally understand

Try making a note of each time you use the word 'sorry', when there is no need to apologize, in a single day.

Write it in this box:

Now try consciously to avoid using the word 'sorry' as much as you can over the next week. Each day, count the number of times you say it and see if you can make the numbers go gradually downwards. (It's not easy, but it gets easier with practice.)

Situations in which I've accidentally blurted out the word 'sorry' without really meaning to in the past week:

- When a guy leapt on the tube before allowing me to get off
- When my friend spilled her coffee all over my sofa
- When a taxi arrived late
- When someone happened to catch my eye as I took a particularly large swallow of wine
- When I accidentally turned off the toilet light from outside while someone else was having a wee (that one was probably justified though)

It's something we don't even think about – and it can start to creep into all the areas of our lives, from the way we interact in public spaces, to the way we act in relationships, to the way we behave in interviews or in the classroom.

And it's not just the word 'sorry', it's the attitude that goes along with it. The attitude that says: I'm probably in the wrong, it's my mistake, let me get out of your way, don't worry, I'll take the blame, it's my fault, *sorry, sorry, sorry, sorry, sorry.*

So how does this have an impact on our lives?

Well, when it comes to careers, studies suggest that how confident we feel about our own abilities can have a major impact at every level, from the likelihood that we'll even apply for a job in the first place, to the way we present ourselves in the interview, to the salary we negotiate, to whether we ask for promotions.

For example, according to a widely-quoted senior executive at

Hewlett Packard, one internal study at the company found that women will only apply for a job if they meet 100 per cent of the stated job requirements, while men will apply if they meet just 60 per cent. In fact, men are *so* much more confident about applying when they don't fit the full criteria that when one university advertised a women-only position, THIRTY men applied for the job.

And, of course, there are comparable experiences before we reach the point of careers – from applying for internships or work experience to auditioning for a show or going for a spot on the college newspaper.

At a day-to-day level, this is the sort of thing that translates into being less likely to ask teachers for their time and extra help, raising your hand less often in class and so on.

So it does matter. These things all impact on one another. Writing for the college newspaper might help you land an internship which might lead to a career in journalism.

Take this simple quiz to see if you might need to boost your confidence:

1. In a science class, the teacher asks a question that you're 80 per cent sure you know the answer to.
Do you:
a) Wait to see if anyone else puts their hand up first, before tentatively raising yours
b) Wave your hands in the air and shout, 'I KNOW I KNOW I KNOW'
c) Hide under your desk and say nothing

2. You get back an assignment you had worked really hard on, and are disappointed to see you got a C grade when you'd thought it was worth an A.

Do you:

a) Ask the teacher to go through it with you and point out how you can improve

b) Demand a re-mark and chain yourself to the staff lounge until your teacher agrees out of sheer embarrassment

c) Burn it in shame under the full moon

3. You're down to the last two candidates for editor of a student magazine.

Do you:

a) Stay up all night preparing a portfolio of your previous work and practising interview questions

b) Sneak into your rival's desk and replace his sample articles with pages ripped out of *My Little Pony* weekly

c) Start preparing yourself to take up the position of deputy editor with a smile

If you scored mostly 'a's: You're on the right track, but you could afford to be a little bit more confident at times

If you scored mostly 'b's: Excellent work, keep it up (maybe tone it down juuuust a *smidge*)

If you scored mostly 'c's: Come on now. Are you a girl or a kitten? If you're a kitten, awesome reading skills. If you're a girl, you need to girl up! Work on being a bit more assertive, speaking up and asking for what you deserve.

People who talk louder sound like they know more. People who say things with confidence are more likely to be trusted. People who undermine themselves are giving other people reasons to doubt them.

This doesn't mean we all have to be super confident all the time. And I'm not saying you have to 'bluster it out' if you're experiencing discrimination, or sexism, or unfairness – we should shout about those things at the top of our voices and demand justice.

It just means through it all we have to try our hardest to back ourselves, and to be on our own team. You'll come up against other people who might try to criticize or put you down, so you need to be kind to yourself and believe in your own talents, whatever they are.

One of the reasons girls don't always feel 'qualified' or able to take certain career routes is that they don't hear about women doing those jobs.

In 2014, I went into a school to talk to young children aged seven to eight about careers. I started out by asking them to close their eyes and imagine they were at the dentist. I told them to imagine the green walls and the big chair, the bright light shining in their eyes and the minty smell. Then I told them to imagine that the door opened and the dentist walked in. With their eyes still closed, I asked them to put up their hand if the dentist they were seeing was a man. When they opened their eyes and looked around, they realized that almost every single student had automatically imagined a male dentist. It's worth noting, too, that if I had asked them more ques-tions, I would probably have heard that they were mostly imagining a white, middle-aged, non-disabled, heterosexual, cisgender (not trans) dentist! We don't tend to think of this as a big deal, but it matters that the person we think of when we think 'human' reflects these societal defaults, as if being a woman, or gay, or disabled is like an extra piece that you clip on top of the regular 'white man' Lego figure. This matters, because when we think of just one type of person as the 'natural' or 'normal' starting point for humanity, we are unconsciously suggesting something about everybody who doesn't fall into that category – they are secondary, extra, deviant, strange, abnormal ... and that can have a real impact on the way people are treated without us even realizing it.

Next, I asked them some questions about what jobs they felt they were suited to. Here are some of the actual things they said:

'Girls can't be airline pilots because you have to be really good at maths and girls make too many mistakes.'

'Girls can't be firefighters or ambulance workers because you have to be really brave.'

'Girls have two choices really – hairdressing or fashion.'

'Men can be doctors but girls are usually nurses.'

There are brilliant, challenging jobs for girls in the beauty and fashion industries for sure, but I hated the idea that these young girls already felt they only had two choices, while their male class-mates came out with a wide and varied list of jobs they thought they could choose from.

So in the interests of giving you some inspiration for smash-ing glass ceilings and generally hitting it out of the park, here's some real-life advice straight from the horses' mouths, or rather, straight from the mouths of some incredible, ass-kicking women who have excelled in often challenging or male-dominated spheres.

Mary Beard, Professor of Classics at the University of Cambridge, Royal Academy of Arts Professor of Ancient Literature, award-win-ning writer, TV presenter (and so damn modest that when I asked for her job title she just said 'university teacher')

1. What advice would you give to a young woman wanting to succeed in the career path you have taken? ·

Don't be taken in by those who make the most noise ... And one sign of success is when you open your mouth and you hear yourself speaking, and you are not pretending to be someone else.

2. If you could go back, what would you like to tell your teenage self?

It's OK to be anxious, uncertain and unconfident (do we actually like people who aren't?). But don't turn it in on yourself.

Shami Chakrabarti, former Director of Liberty (2003–16), Chancellor of the University of Essex

1. What advice would you give to a young woman wanting to succeed in the career path you have taken?

Be bold, be fearless, don't undersell yourself and don't let the naysayers get you down. If you dedicate yourself to campaigning, there will always be those who don't like what you say, or have a vested interest in criticizing you. In today's world, that's a growing challenge for women and girls – look at the aggressive, misogynistic trolling of our most high-profile feminist activists on social media. It can be bruising, but if you truly believe in what you're doing, and the change it can make, you can steel yourself against it.

Even in the voluntary sector, where the majority of the workforce are women, men still dominate the leadership roles. That's changing, but it's important to remember that no woman is an island – we must help each other to make sure it changes for good. Since starting out in my career, I've been lucky enough to benefit from the kindness, encouragement, advice and solidarity of more senior women, and I consider it a responsibility to do the same for younger colleagues, and potential colleagues. I try to surround myself with people who inspire me, challenge me and whose opinion and expertise I trust – and not a day goes by when I don't learn something new.

Finally, don't pressure yourself to know the direction you

want your life to take straight away, or compare yourself to those people who seem to take over the world before they turn twenty! Mark Zuckerberg and Bill Gates are the anomalies, not the norm. Most people spend years working in different areas before they find the role that's the best fit for them – I know I did – but they don't tell you that at school! Liberty is full of people from a wide range of backgrounds – barristers, journalists, civil servants, all sorts – and that diversity of experience is one of our biggest strengths. Don't worry about what you feel people expect you to do. Do what feels best for you.

2. If you could go back, what would you like to tell your teenage self?

If I met my younger self now, I think I'd find her quite precocious! I'd advise her that you can be confident without being arrogant, and angry without being combative, I'd tell her not to be afraid to take risks – and I'd pass on the motto I live by nowadays: everyone's equal, no one's superior.

Paris Lees, *VICE* columnist, *Attitude* magazine Editor-at-Large, television personality, transgender activist

1. What advice would you give to a young woman wanting to succeed in the career path you have taken?

This isn't an easy question to answer as I was very privileged to have been in a stable relationship with someone who financially supported me while I established myself in the media. I was lucky. It's very hard to break into journalism without support like this, or the support of your family, but if you do have somewhere to live, all I can say is write. Write, write, write. About whatever and whoever it is that you are passionate about, because otherwise what's the point? And don't give up! Remember to ask to be paid too. If someone asks you to write something, it is not only perfectly acceptable to politely ask, 'How much do you offer for pieces like this?', it is utterly necessary. No one is going to hand life's riches out to you on a plate so remember that your time and your work and you are worth something. Oh, and remember to have fun, too. Career success is great, but there's more to life than work.

2. If you could go back, what would you like to tell your teenage self?

Please, please, please understand how wonderful and perfect you are just as you are. You don't need to buy a product to change the colour of your skin. You don't need to buy a product to make your eyelashes thicker. You don't need to wear shoes that hurt you just because they make you look a little taller. If you want to do those things, fine, but remember that dressing up is meant to be fun, not compulsory. What you need to be doing now is having fun, and reading, and trying new experiences. You will never get your teenage years back and you won't look back and wish you'd spent more time shaving your legs instead of exploring the wonderful world that is now your oyster.

Helen Sharpe, Lecturer in Clinical Psychology at the University of Edinburgh

1. What advice would you give to a young woman wanting to succeed in the career path you have taken?

In the academic world (and many others I imagine!) I would say to go and seek out opportunities, don't wait for them to come to you. Having someone who can help steer you through the process is hugely valuable, so you need to find people who you respect and who are fun to be around and find a way to work with them.

2. If you could go back, what would you like to tell your teenage self?

Do what you enjoy. You may not end up earning as much as other people or 'making it' in the formal sense, but most of your adult waking life is spent at work so it's more important than you can imagine to be able to get up in the morning and feel like you want to go. I would also say: don't rush. You may feel like you need to be on a career path from age eighteen but many of my friends who do the most interesting and fulfilling work only came to it five or ten years down the line.

Ellie Cosgrave, engineer, research associate, Director of ScienceGrrl

1. What advice would you give to a young woman wanting to succeed in the career path you have taken?

Don't be afraid to ask for help, advice or mentorship; no one is expected to know everything. Most people will be flattered to be asked and delighted to be able to help. Asking questions demonstrates that you are inquisitive, motivated, passionate and brave – it also means you get to learn stuff!

2. If you could go back, what would you like to tell your teenage self?

The things about yourself that you think make you weird are actually the things that make you really special. Never let anyone make you feel small, inadequate or silly for doing something you believe in.

Zena White, Managing Director, The Other Hand record label services

1. What advice would you give to a young woman wanting to succeed in the career path you have taken?

There are a lot of people in the music industry who are self-taught as experience is considered more valuable than formal training. I would recommend choosing companies you work for carefully and finding smart teachers or mentors who you can learn from at every stage of your career. Never be afraid to say you don't know or to speak up when you have a different opinion, and always treat others with respect, even when you disagree. It is a small industry and reputation is very important.

2. If you could go back, what would you like to tell your teenage self?

Ha! I would tell my younger self that success doesn't come quickly or easily and hard work pays off. Also in my experience success isn't defined by what other people think of you, it's defined by what you think of yourself and the integrity with which you carry out your work.

Anita Anand, journalist, broadcaster and author

1. What advice would you give to a young woman wanting to succeed in the career path you have taken?

It's hard but it is so rewarding. If you like asking questions and like questioning answers, then journalism is for you. If you just want to be on telly or the radio, then this is probably not the route I would recommend; the road is long and you step it story by story. Newsrooms are hectic places and editors among the most harassed members of society, so if you are going for a job/placement it's good to have your pitch sorted early. Decide what kind of journalism you like, the writers you admire and devour the genre. Also get involved early. I worked on the school magazine, and the college paper. That meant when I went for interviews I already had cuttings to show in the five minutes I was given to prove myself. You have so many opportunities to be 'out there' early. When I ran a newsroom, I looked for young people who were interested in their world and were developing a 'voice' – blogging is a great way to show both.

2. If you could go back, what would you like to tell your teenage self?

Be confident but don't bullshit. Honestly, sometimes I look back and cringe ... Nobody expects a sixteen-year-old to have all the answers to everything ... but somehow I thought I should always have something pithy and wise to say ... I wish I had learned the sentence 'I don't know the answer but I know where to find it' a lot earlier. It would have saved so much time/argument and embarrassment.

Josie Long, comedian, activist, force of nature

1. What advice would you give to a young woman wanting to succeed in the career path you have taken?

Please don't waste even a second of your time or energy engaging with sexist debates. I have spent most of my life being dragged into two pointless faux-debates, these being:

1. Can women be funny/Are women funny? (Answer: yes)

2. Why are there no funny women/successful TV women? (Answer: there are, and there would be even more if the people making things were less sexist)

If anyone asks you either of these questions or tells you these things as if they are fact, then do not hesitate in shutting them down. They aren't worth your time. You don't need to convince anyone why you're allowed or able to do this and you certainly aren't to blame for sexist bookers/commissioners etc. It's noise and don't let it drain even a drop of your energy. Tell them you're not interested in the conversation. Tell them they are being sexist in hinting you can't do/shouldn't do/aren't already doing your job.

If you're aiming to do TV: pitch all of the time and pitch to be the star of the show. Far too many shows in comedy are far too male-skewed and it's the fault of the people making them, so provide them with as many brilliant chances to make something great that you can. Redress the balance.

So please, ignore the bullshit and call out sexism for what it is – unacceptable, not your fault and in fact nothing to do with you.

If you ever receive abuse online, don't suffer in silence, you don't have to rise above it – someone else is behaving unacceptably and they need to stop. Not you! Don't let anyone silence you.

But most of all: make your own kind of comedy, do exactly the kind of thing that develops your own comic voice and do it loud and proud and all of the time. Comedy needs your voices, dammit!

2. If you could go back, what would you like to tell your teenage self?

I would tell myself that every time you're told by an interviewer that 'there aren't any funny women, are there?' you're allowed to say 'Shut. The. Fuck. Up.'

I also used to cling to relationships because I came from a bit of a troubled background, so I would say to my younger self: be single, be free and live your whole life for yourself without feeling the need to have a boyfriend the whole time. Be a whole person!

Martha Lane Fox, Baroness of Soho, co-founder of LastMinute.com

1. What advice would you give to a young woman wanting to succeed in the career path you have taken?
My career has been very strange – from entrepreneurialism to politics. If it shows anything then it's that you can span public and private, and for profit/not for profit – don't be held back by definitions or boundaries.

2. If you could go back, what would you like to tell your teenage self?
One thing very specific – on 2 May 2004, wear your seatbelt.
    One thing less so – don't waste time beating yourself up about not doing enough/being good enough.

Dr Bettany Hughes, award-winning historian, author, broadcaster

1. What advice would you give to a young woman wanting to succeed in the career path you have taken?
I was told very firmly that I was mad to pursue a career in history; at the time the study of the past was deeply unfashionable. But I knew that understanding the story of humanity really mattered – so against the odds and against all advice I pursued my passion. My history programmes are now watched by 250 million viewers a year – you know in your heart what is right. So I would say never take no for an answer!

2. If you could go back, what would you like to tell your teenage self?

Every cell in your teenage body tells you to experience all the world has to offer right now – just relax a bit, you have a lifetime to love, live, learn. The most important thing about teenage years is to be a good friend and to learn what true friendship means – we are never alone in the world. Soak up experiences but give yourself time to think, and remember, live wisely and well and the world is yours.

Charlotte Cray, editorial assistant at the Borough Press

1. What advice would you give to a young woman wanting to succeed in the career path you have taken?

Do something you very much like, with something you love up ahead and then face squarely towards it. I found out fast that I couldn't work in an industry that didn't like me and that I didn't like. Publishing is a business, yes, but it is the book business, and thus mostly full of nerds whose devotion to the written word is both sentimental and implacable. I like that combination.

Prepare to be terrible at your job for a while, learning is the worst and the best; nothing is worth doing if it is easy. The moment it's effortless (I will relish the day) throw yourself back in the deep end. Your career should be forged by you – make a move.

2. If you could go back, what would you like to tell your teenage self?

Earn your own respect. It takes ages, it's a constant and worthy battle and it's by far the hardest to win. Also, youthful Charlotte, don't worry, there's no prize-giving at the end. No one comes first, so ignore what everyone else is doing and do what makes your eyes light up and makes you not able to stop talking.

Don't wait for people to invite you to take part. Politely volunteer yourself. You like learning on your feet – so stand up.

Listen to your own advice. One of the more important and regular pieces of advice I give myself these days is that you don't have to take everyone's advice. Get as much information as you can from whomever is open enough to offer it to you, but know when to listen to yourself above all others – it's your life.

Nimco Ali, anti-FGM activist, co-founder of Daughters of Eve

1. The fear of failing is fully worse than doing so. And when you let go you will find that you are stronger than you could have imagined! So don't wait until you are thirty, do it now!

2. Study what you love and do what fulfils you. Success is not what you find in your bank account but in the deeds around you.

Justine Roberts, founder of Mumsnet and Gransnet

1. What advice would you give to a young woman wanting to succeed in the career path you have taken?

The trick to going it alone and setting up your own company is to be really passionate about something. If you truly believe it's going to be useful or solve a problem, you can be much more confident about going for it, and you'll be much more likely to keep going when you have inevitable setbacks.

Then, once you're up and running, make sure you consult

with and listen to your audience all the way. It's easy to become wedded to an idea, but you need to be able to pivot, and in the world of social media, feedback is immediate and constant. At Mumsnet, we're lucky to have a 24/7 focus group full of clever, opinionated women willing to give us free advice; critical feedback may be galling at the time, but it creates an opportunity to refine and hone what you do and, if necessary, to change direction. Adaptability is vital. Oh, and it helps if you're doing something you love; it makes it easier to get up in the morning.

2. If you could go back, what would you like to tell your teenage self?

Have confidence in your own ideas. Growing up, there was an unwritten rule in my family that if you were 'one of us' you were organized but uncreative. So it came as a surprise to learn that I did have ideas – admittedly, half of them are crap, but some are not. People may give you a label or you may even label yourself, but you should always give yourself opportunities to challenge them.

Samira Ahmed, BBC presenter, *Celebrity Mastermind* winner

1. What advice would you give to a young woman wanting to succeed in the career path you have taken?

Yes, it is sexist. Yes, it is racist. But you have to persevere. Keep at it. Focus on being better than the others and taking it one step at a time. Find supportive people; there are lots out there. And be generous in return. Don't be afraid to reassess what you think you want every so often. But don't quit. Just pace yourself and pick your battles.

2. If you could go back, what would you like to tell your teenage self?

Don't throw out all those issues of *Jackie* magazine. I wish I'd kept them. Don't waste all that time worrying about how you look. You look fine. Seriously. I can't believe how much time I wasted. In fact, master time management. Not in a stupid career advice manual way, just think about how you want to spend that time. With people you really like or books you want to re-read. Being happy in your own company is so important. Otherwise I would say, you were right to focus on the world beyond school. Get the best grades you can and get out and on with your life. It gets so much better.

Bridget Christie, stand-up comedian, writer, actor

1. What advice would you give to a young woman wanting to succeed in the career path you have taken?

It's a boring old cliché, but there really is no other way to be a good stand-up other than hard graft. Get as much stage-time as you can and don't be impatient. Try not to worry about bad gigs as they will be the making of you. Don't imagine you have to be like someone else in order to achieve great things, but be the best version of yourself. Most importantly, don't be intimidated or put off by sexist comments, be encouraged by them.

2. If you could go back, what would you like to tell your teenage self?

This is the worst time of your life. Get through it. The rest is going to be fucking ace.

*

Notice how many of these absolutely amazing, ass-kicking women make the point of telling their teenage self that it's all up from here? That's no coincidence. Even the most incredible, successful women often had a crappy time earlier on. But this roll call of literal awesomeness is the proof that you really can girl up, give no fucks, shake it off and go on to break boundaries and shatter expectations. They all did it and you can too.

All this might seem a bit far away and daunting, but you would be amazed at how many young people find ingenious and successful ways to jump-start their own careers. Take Tavi Gevinson, who started her career with a fashion blog aged just twelve and launched her own magazine at fifteen. Or June Eric Udorie, who threw herself into feminist activism with organizations like Plan and Youth for Change and became such a well-respected campaigner that she was asked to start writing for the *New Statesmen* aged just sixteen.

Notice how these stories often involve digital technology? If you want to give yourself a fab skillset and a career-boosting head start, learning to code is a great idea, and it's much easier than you might think! Check out some of the programs on offer from organizations like Girls Who Code, Vidcode, Girl Develop It, or Black Girls Code. Or learn online with free programs like Scratch or Code Academy, or in a fun game setting with Code Racer. And while we're on the subject, if you're interested in STEM (science, technology, engineering or mathematics), check out the amazing Stemettes or find a ScienceGrrl chapter near you (info in the back of the book).

TOP 5 CAREER TIPS

1. Practice makes perfect

Whatever it is you love doing, do it again and again until you're brilliant at it. Whether you want to be a mathematician, a musician or a journalist, find ways to get as much experience as you possibly can, and build up a portfolio of your work that you can show to potential future employers.

2. Ask for advice

Don't ever be afraid to reach out and ask for help. The worst thing people can say is no. The internet has made it possible to get in contact with people at the click of a mouse – find leaders in your field, find potential employers, find role models and ask them for advice, for opportunities, for mentoring. You never know where it might lead.

3. Put yourself out there

Join a group, apply for the school play or band, enter a competition, go for an internship – whatever it takes, the first step towards getting paid to do what you love is to just start doing it. If writing is what you love, start a blog and update it regularly. If you want to be a TV presenter, start a YouTube channel and start building up a following.

What's the worst that could happen? OK, you could accidentally end up recording yourself miming along to One Direction in your underwear using your hairbrush as a microphone and upload it to the internet by mistake when you thought you were uploading a blog post, and then it could make the national press and get picked up by BuzzFeed and the actual Harry Styles might tweet about it and you'd try and do an interview to set the record straight but then get so nervous that you throw up live on air.

But how likely is that really?

(If this has actually happened to you, you get a free pass and don't have to put yourself out there. Also, my condolences.)

4. You can change your mind

It's OK not to be sure yet about what it is that you want to do. It's also OK to have one idea firmly in your head for years and then decide that actually you're going to do something else. People are sometimes scared to change goals or paths because they think it looks like giving up, or being a coward. It's actually the bravest thing in the world to walk away from something safe and familiar towards something scary and unknown. (Just look at Betty Boothroyd, who started out as a dancer in the Tiller Girls troupe but ended up becoming an MP and the only ever female Speaker of the House of Commons. Good job she wasn't too scared to take a leap of faith.)

5. Keep on going!

Remember that not succeeding, whether it's in an interview or an application, doesn't mean you're a failure. It just means you're another step closer to where you're going.

It's an old cliché, but there's some truth in the fact that what doesn't kill you makes you stronger. Recovering and learning from rejection can help us to work out our best points and our weaknesses. Having to keep on trying also makes success even sweeter when it finally arrives.

The world is chockfull of incredibly successful people who didn't make it the first time – like J. K. Rowling, complete and utter shero and one of the most successful writers in the history of the universe. Her first book was rejected by twelve publishers before being bought by Bloomsbury. Or legendary *Vogue* editor Anna Wintour, who was fired from *Harper's Bazaar* after nine months for being too 'edgy'. Hell, even Steven Spielberg was rejected from the University of Southern California School of Theater, Film and Television a whopping three times. And his films aren't exactly bad. (Well, apart from *Indiana Jones and the Kingdom of the Crystal Skull* but everyone's allowed an off-day.)

✳

Finally, remember that like any challenge, gaining the kind of skills and knowledge you need for your chosen career is easier with help and support. Many schools and universities should have a careers department where you can go to ask about options and get started early on, building up the kind of skills and experience you need to proceed. Remember that extra-curricular activities from sport to volunteering can all help to boost your CV and demonstrate transferable skills for the future, like leadership and teamwork. It's never too soon to start.

Friends can also go a long way supporting each other. One of the most inspiring teenage girls I've ever met was a young student who had decided she wanted to apply to study medicine at university, but found the application process and the amount of hoops she needed to jump through complicated and daunting. Instead of giving up, she set up a club at her school where students who wanted to apply for medicine could get together after school and support one another through the process, helping each other to complete applications and study for tests.

Once you've succeeded in getting a position, a summer job or a spot on a committee, you might be able to use your platform to help promote another young woman, whether it's by putting her in touch with a contact or helping her to apply for a position.

Remember, it's not just about smashing the glass ceiling; it's about passing on your hammer to the next girl. And if you have a moment, consider whacking a ladder in there, would you?

CHAPTER SEVEN

SLUTS, UNICORNS AND OTHER MYTHICAL CREATURES

There is no such thing as a slut. It belongs in this list of things that don't exist:

- Fairies
- Minotaurs
- Unicorns
- Centaurs
- Dragons
- Sluts
- Slags
- Whores
- Robin Thicke's sex appeal

A 'slut' isn't a type of girl. 'Slut' is an attitude projected onto girls and women by a sexist society that is alarmed when they take control and make their own decisions. Until quite recently, 'slut' was used as a negative term for women who outrageously neglected female duties like sweeping and cleaning and had messy houses. Now it's used to express panic at the idea of women who dare to enjoy sex and decide how much they want and who they want it with. The same goes for a whore or a slag or a tramp or a floozy or a skank or a sket or a ho. Unless you're using a hoe to tend your marigolds, none of these things exist. Basically they're just words we use to describe a girl who does what a guy would be called a 'legend', 'lad', 'stud' or 'player' for doing.

A slut isn't a person, it's in the eye of the beholder. Like beauty, or an annoying eyelash. We decide who a girl is based on something she's done (or even just rumoured to have done) and then brand her with it as if it's a permanent part of her identity. Guys, on the other hand, get to wear their relationships and 'conquests' like medals or badges of honour, which are much easier to take off, and hurt a lot less.

In fact, when you think about it, we have a million ways to label girls as too sexy or not sexy enough . . . and there's only the tiniest space in the middle where your behaviour is deemed 'acceptable'.

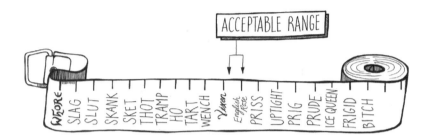

But who you are isn't who you date, or who you've slept with. Imagine if we decided someone's whole identity could be determined by another random action, like having cornflakes for breakfast. That would just be weird. It's pretty stupid and we need to stop doing it. But the only way to change something like how we judge people is from inside the system that's judging them. So it'll only stop happening if we all step up. Don't let people 'slut-shame' a girl in front of you, don't pass on rumours or gossip about someone else's relationship and just let people have whatever cereal they want, OK?

Relationships don't define you.

They can be:

Amazing
Fulfilling
Enriching
Beautiful

But they aren't:

Your identity
The only way to be happy
A magic wand
A measure of your success
Much like the movies
OK, at all like the movies

And not being in one does *not* automatically make you:

A failure
Desperate
Sad
Unlovable
Incomplete

This might all seem pretty obvious. But there's a reason it needs to be said. We live in a world that sends a very powerful message, to everybody, but particularly to women and girls, that finding 'Mr Right', your 'prince', your 'soulmate', your 'knight in shining armour' is the ultimate success. We learn from an incredibly young age that the main goal of a woman's life is to find a man to settle down with, to look after her, to father the children she (obviously) wants.

Think about Disney princesses, romantic comedies, Ikea adverts ... Hell, even the emoticons on your Smartphone (apart from the little smiley poop that is everybody's favourite) are mainly about the importance of snuggling, getting engaged, marrying, cosying up and having babies ...

Boys get these messages too, but not to the same extent. As a society, we treat women who are un-partnered at a certain age very differently from men. Think about the way the media has treated Jennifer Aniston (poor, lonely, desperate, tragically child-less) compared to George Clooney (sexy, eligible, improves with age). When he got married, the headlines were all about how lucky his (ass-kicking internationally renowned barrister) wife was, but when she did, they were all about how she finally snagged a man.

Just think of the difference in the connotations of the words 'bach-elor' and 'spinster'. There is no male equivalent for the phrase 'left on the shelf'.

We often see both men and women portrayed as being fulfilled by a relationship in a movie. But in the majority of films starring men, the girl is a sort of side-attraction, like a bonus score on the way to achieving the actual goal, which is the main part of the movie's plot – like saving the world, or blowing up the bad guy, or finding the treasure, or all three (not that realistic, guys). On the other hand, in films where women are the central characters, the story very often revolves around the central focus of finding and keeping a man. Or starting her own cupcake bakery. Or both. (More realistic, slightly depressing.) So we get the message that while relationships are important status symbols for men, they are the single most important achievement for women.

We also often get the message that a woman is defined by her relationship, in a way that isn't necessarily true for men – think footballers' wives and girlfriends, or WAGS, first ladies, royal women or 'real housewives'. Their very identity is perceived to be wrapped up in the man they are attached to, whereas those men have quite separate identities, careers and achievements of their own in addition to their relationships.

Even when we look at a much younger age group, boys who choose not to have relationships at school are often portrayed as focused, sporty, or just not 'having time for all that drama'. Girls, on the other hand, are more often painted as desperate, losers, or failures if they don't manage to 'snare' a boyfriend, partly because of the assumption that that must surely be their constant goal. The idea that a girl might just not be interested in romance, might want to focus on other things, or might be more interested in girls than in guys doesn't really seem to cross anybody's mind.

We also have the strange idea that girls and guys are completely different in how they approach relationships or behave in them. We act like girls can't think of anything else but guys have more important things on their minds. We act like girls are supposed to be brilliant at understanding everything that's going on and guys are totally clueless about how to talk about emotional stuff. We act like girls are clingy and guys need their space.

For example, when Zayn Malik left One Direction, there was an outpouring of fan anger against his fiancée Perrie Edwards. People were drawing on the stereotype of the clingy, needy, insecure girlfriend, even though Edwards is an international music star in her own right with a massive career touring with Little Mix. The idea that she'd want Zayn sitting at home without her literally makes no sense at all. She wouldn't even be at home, guys. She's got stadium tours to complete and records to smash. She'd be all like: 'Hey Zayn, have an awesome time playing Xbox, I'll see you in six months, yeah?' But imagine if she had dropped out of Little Mix while he stayed in One Direction – people wouldn't have been shouting about Zayn being responsible, they would probably have been guessing that she was feeling broody, or ready to settle down. There are a lot of false ideas about relationships that we've heard so often we assume them to be true even though they're not.

False facts about relationships

- Girls are needy and insecure
- Guys never get insecure
- Guys are always cheating
- Girls are scheming and manipulate their partners
- Relationships always have to be full of drama
- It's sweet or romantic to be jealous
- Girls are all into guys and guys are all into girls
- It's not a real relationship without sex
- A guy should never see you without your make-up on
- You're either straight or gay and there are no other options
- Being in a relationship makes you cooler than someone who isn't
- It's more important than your friends
- It means never having to say sorry for farting

Basically a whole load of rubbish is talked about relationships. You should always say sorry for farting.

Some things people have made up about relationships that are total bollocks include the 'friend zone', being a 'cock-tease' and the idea that the type of relationship depends on the sexuality of the people in it.

SPOILER ALERT:

"Friend
zoning"...

NOT A REAL THING

The 'friend zone' isn't a thing. If you haven't heard of it, it's the idea that a guy who is 'too nice' to a girl and doesn't make a move immediately can end up becoming too good a friend for her to think of him romantically. Because of that thing where girls never get together with guys they've previously been friends with. Except that they do. All the time.

Anyway, eventually he tells her how he feels, but she says she won't date him because their friendship is too important to her and she wouldn't want to risk it. He's in the 'friend zone'. BOOM.

Except that whoever came up with this theory has made several WHOPPING errors:

1. When someone says they don't want to risk the friendship, it's almost always a nice way of letting you down gently. There aren't girls all over the world who are desperately in love with their male friends but refusing to let themselves try a relationship. If they fancy you that much, they'll risk it. She's not interested, dude. Take a hint.

2. Being nice to a girl is important if you like her. Becoming her friend isn't some massive mistake because dammit you should have been shitting all over her if you wanted a shot at getting her to go out with you. #MassiveLogicFail

3. Girls don't *owe* guys sex just for being nice. Seriously, fuck off.

See also: cock-tease (a girl who has the nerve to be nice to a guy or even flirt with him and then not shag him. I *know*, right? What an outrageous bitch). A girl has every right to decide she doesn't want to have sex with you at any time, period.

(Also while she's on her period, if she doesn't feel like it. Period.

Alternatively, it's totally fine to have sex on your period if you do want to but you might not feel like it if you're going through one of those crampy period periods. Period.)

The only time you're a cock-tease is if you're standing in front of a naked guy, tickling his penis and saying to it: 'You're a bit of a silly cock, aren't you? Oh, not really, I'm only teasing.'

And another whopping myth is the idea that a 'gay relationship' is somehow completely different from a 'straight relationship'. We're just people, y'all. There's as much variation between choices and speeds and types of relationship as there are people, whoever's bumping and grinding with whom, and whatever their sexual orientation or gender identity. Being pansexual means you're attracted to people of any sex or gender identity. It doesn't mean you automatically have a greater appetite for sex. Being bisexual means you're attracted to both men and women. It isn't a 'phase', and it doesn't mean you're easy, confused, indecisive, or want a threesome. Nor does it mean you're more likely to cheat. Being transgender means that your gender identity doesn't match the sex you were assigned at birth, and being gender fluid or gender queer might mean that you feel your gender doesn't fit into any single category, or varies over time. But none of these gender categories dictates who you'll fancy. Being a lesbian doesn't mean you're performing your sexuality just to turn on guys. Being gay doesn't mean you move faster in relationships. These are all just ignorant myths. Note: asking a gay couple (of any gender) 'who's the man and who's the woman?' is about as stupid as asking a heterosexual couple 'do you often pretend to be the same sex?'

It's kind of not surprising that we start to believe some of these misconceptions, given how widespread they are. We get confusing messages about relationships from all over the place.

Sometimes it's just subtle and annoying, like those beer adverts about men having to escape their nagging, irritating, awful wives. Sometimes it's full-on, hit-you-in-the-face, shit-your-pants, gob-smackingly awful, like an article *Glamour* magazine published while I was writing this chapter, entitled 'Thirteen Little Things That Can Make a Man Fall Hard for You'. This piece of steaming head-fuckery honest-to-God advised readers to let their man 'help solve your petty work problem', to hand him cold beverages as he gets out of the shower and give him massages, to make him snacks immediately after sex ('a simple grilled cheese or milk and cookies will do'), to answer the door naked, to 'spit' out statistics about his favourite sports team and to sit beside him like a faithful dog while he watches his favourite TV show, even if you don't enjoy it. Because the 1950s just seemed too damn progressive, ladies, so *Glamour* is taking us back to somewhere in the early nineteeth century. (In fairness, they did at least have the decency to delete the article and apologise once this was pointed out to them!)

It's kind of unsurprising that we get confused about relationships when we're living in a world where a mainstream publication can unironically think it's a great idea to tell women they need to act like naked, Stepford robots and treat their partners like spoilt, stupid, sex-crazed infants in order to snare a guy for keeps. Literally get in the sea right now, *Glamour* magazine.

These messages from magazines come thick and fast, and they basically say this:

- Finding a man is every woman's dream and priority
- Once you've bagged one (perhaps literally, using a sack and a rope), somehow tricking him into proposing becomes your immediate number-one priority

- The only way to achieve both of the above is by eating less, buying more, looking better and giving blow jobs

So we end up starting to think that it's all about pleasing the guy, working out how to attract him, moulding ourselves to fit his taste, without stopping for a second to go 'who cares if he's into me, do I even like this guy?' and 'wait, am I even straight?' If you want a relationship but you feel like you never meet anyone 'right', don't panic. It doesn't mean you're unloveable or 'unfanciable'. It probably just means that out of all the immediately surrounding people ... you're the best one. You haven't found anyone awesome enough to deserve you yet, but you will in time. You need to work out which person, of any gender, you really like enough to want to be in a relationship with them, not just start trawling desperately for anyone with a pulse to call your partner. It's not like Hook a Duck. It's not Hook a Dick. And deciding whether to text them doesn't need to be a huge, convoluted game the way some magazine flowchart quizzes suggest either. It's actually pretty simple ...

This constant 'girls must all be desperately seeking boyfriends, all the time' narrative can be scary, or make you feel excluded. Especially if you're having some feelings that are confusing or mixed up, about what kind of person or what sex of person you fancy, if you fancy anyone at all, or how you feel about your own gender identity. Despite being ignored by much of the mainstream media, this is totally normal. Sexuality is fluid – it doesn't have to be cut and dried, fitted into this box or that box, and it's OK to work it out over time. The main thing is not to be freaked out or think there's anything weird or wrong about having those feelings. There absolutely isn't and you're very much not alone.

The trouble with the message that we should all be perfecting ourselves for potential future partners, all the time, is that everything starts to be framed from the point of view of what other people might think of you, instead of what makes you feel happy.

Gradually, we start putting ourselves together like a package deal designed for somebody else. And this includes our so-called 'choices'.

A magazine might present a pretty full-page spread of 'choices' between seventeen different types of lipstick, but you don't notice that 'not wearing lipstick' has slipped off your radar as an option altogether. We're told we can find the right bikini to fit our apple, pear or hourglass figure, but choosing to wear whatever bikini you damn well want doesn't fit in any of the boxed-off categories.

What's cleverly presented as a whole range of options actually becomes a narrow instruction manual about how to 'perform' being a girl or a woman in the right way, disguised as our own personal choice.

IT'S NOT A CHOICE IF a

MAGaZINE
made
it For
YOU

We're presented with other women to measure ourselves against (and fail), and we are asked to judge them against one another too. (Who wore it better? What's in her fridge? Ultimate celeb weight loss wins and fails!) From choosing the perfect make-up look for the office to the right 'summer capsule wardrobe' for a holiday with your friends, we're constantly being told to perform, perform, impress!

And thanks to the clichés and the happy endings and the MAKE YOURSELF PERFECT FOR BOYS narratives, we all end up with the weird idea that we're doing a lot of this for the guys. We cleverly blur together the whole 'we have to look perfect all the time' thing with the 'we have to attract the perfect partner thing' so it becomes 'we have to look perfect in order to attract the perfect partner', which makes it sound like all potential partners are interested in is what we look like and nobody will ever fancy you if you don't follow every single instruction in every single magazine.

This doesn't really add up.

When you think about it, it wouldn't really make sense if looks were the biggest factor in a relationship. Looking at the other person is lovely but I wouldn't say it's the biggest benefit of a relationship. If you do it for too long it gets a little creepy TBH. Company, laughter, support, fun, conversation, foot massages, sofa buddies, getting to eat their food when it's better than what you ordered . . . all of these are major relationship benefits that are largely unrelated to what your partner looks like.

And a lot of the time, it's only you that's worrying about looks, not the other person at all.

A close friend of mine finds that her weight fluctuates quite a lot. A while back she put on a bit of weight, and for weeks she worried and stressed about what her boyfriend was thinking about it and whether he wouldn't find her attractive any more. Finally, she screwed up the courage to ask him about it. He said he honestly couldn't tell the difference at all. What felt like a huge deal to her was literally unnoticeable to him. (And, even if it was, there's no way it would have changed the way he felt about her one bit. Because he's not an arsehole.)

We are not doing any of this for the guys.

And the thing is, even if they did notice, would you really want to be with somebody who is picking you apart and judging you on tiny 'problems' with your body? Are we really saying our bodies are only there to please other people?

Don't be sold the lie that sex is something persistent and aggressive and masculine that eventually 'happens' to girls when they reluctantly let their guard down.

Not every guy is gagging for sex and will keep pestering you until you get worn down into reluctant submission. Don't 'submit' to that guy. He's not a romantic hero, he's a jackass. It's not cute, it's rude.

In the long run, someone who's kind, who makes you laugh and feel good about yourself and who you enjoy spending time with is worth a million hotshot handsome popular douchebags who pressure you, put you down or make you feel insecure.

It's worth finding someone who doesn't 'put up with' your choices and your quirks. Don't even consider someone who makes you feel bad about who you are. You want someone who actively celebrates you. You want to find the partner who thinks it's fucking brilliant that you dip your chips in apple juice and make that weird snorting noise while you brush your teeth.

That's the person you want in your corner. The one who celebrates who you are and your life choices, and feels lucky to have you, not the one who criticizes you or makes you feel small.

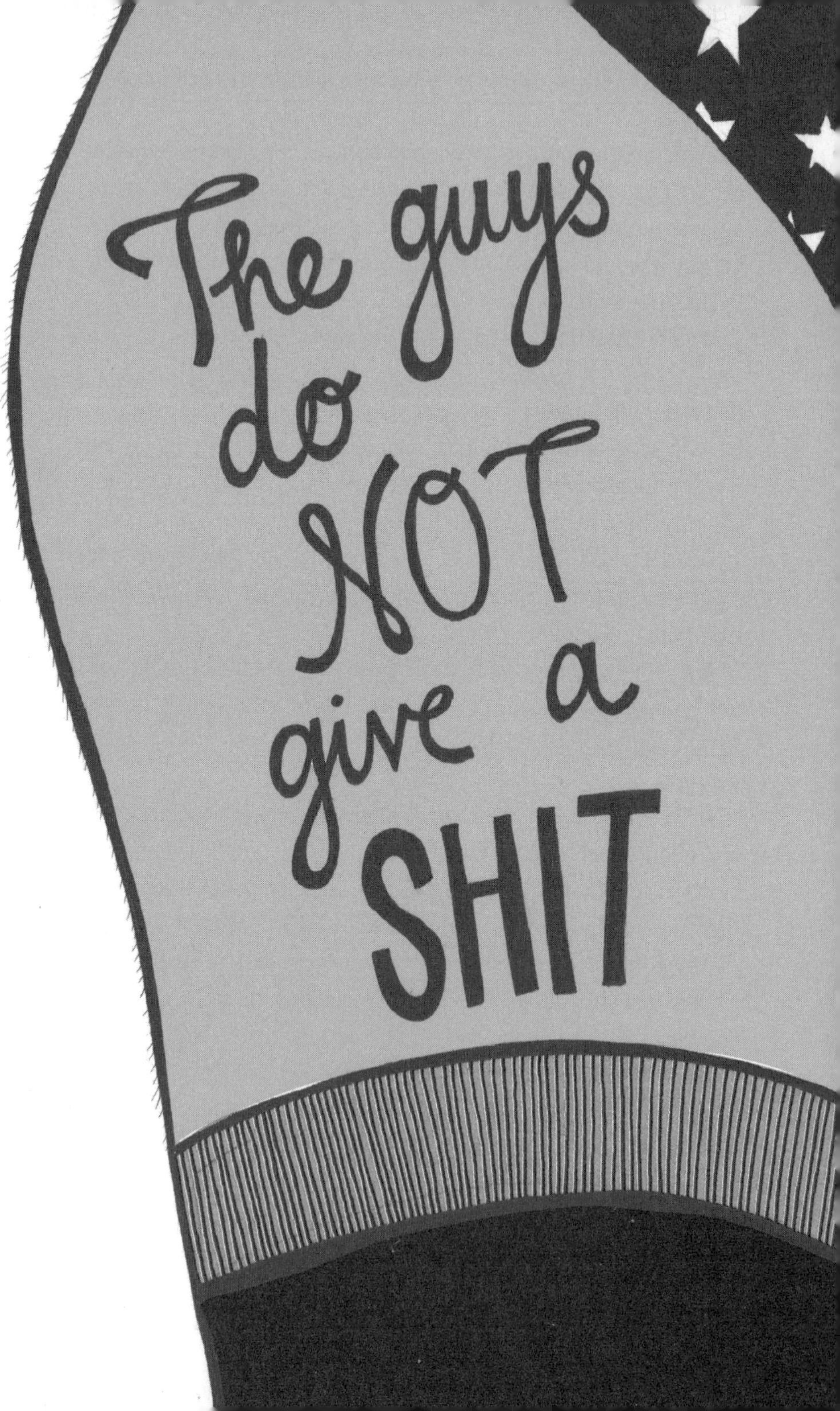
The guys
do
NOT
give a
SHIT

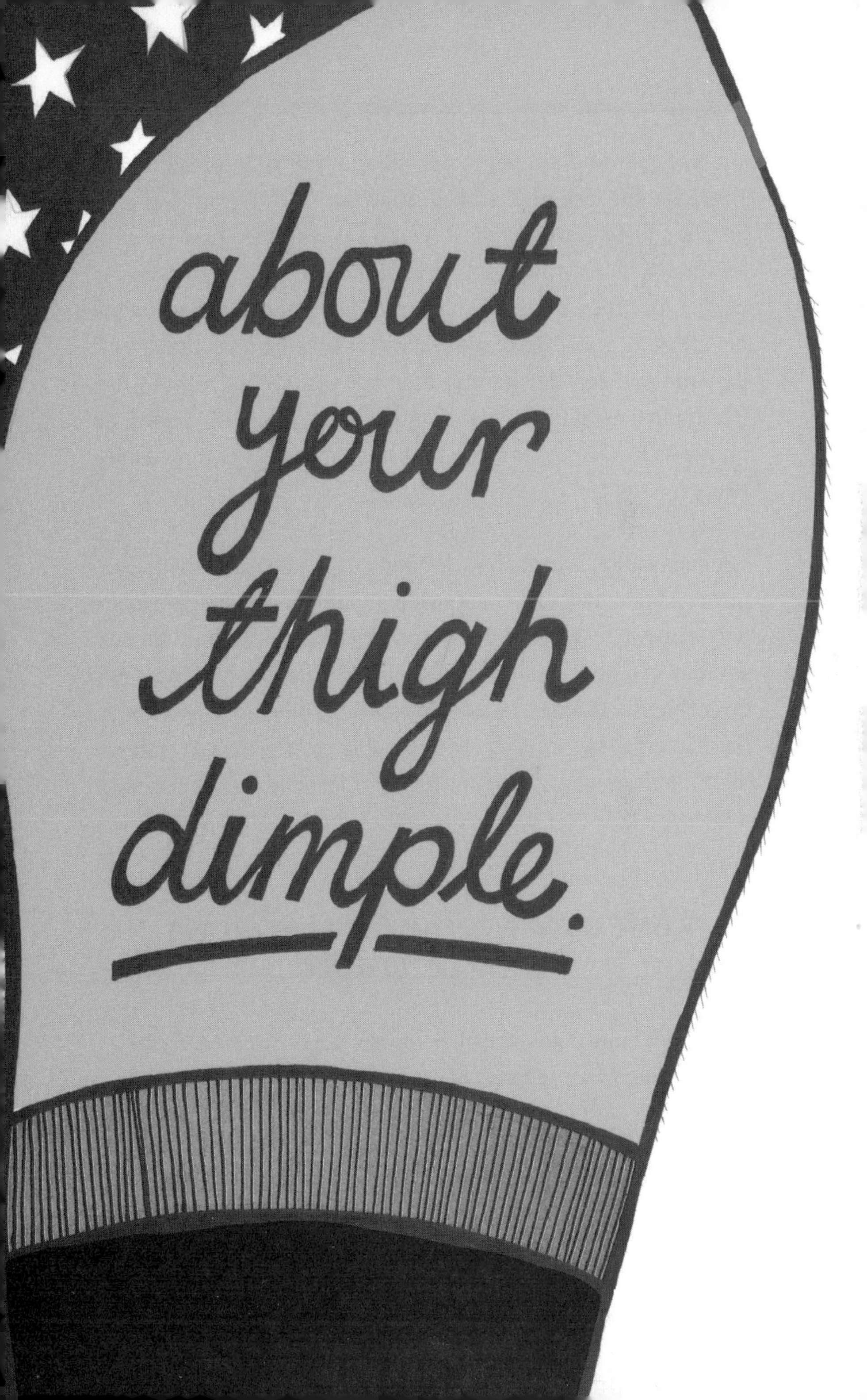
about your thigh dimple.

Once you find someone you like (if you're interested in a relationship), the next stages of awkward conversations and nervous flirting and trying to work out whether they like you and practically throwing up in your mouth just *thinking* about asking them out are terrifying and brilliant and awful and wonderful all at once. Be brave. Be honest. Remember they're as nervous and terrified as you are. Ask yourself how the other person makes you feel and be guided by whether it's good or above on the happy-and-confident scale. Take your time. Enjoy every moment.

Communication is probably the single most important thing for a positive and enjoyable relationship. It nourishes the relationship and helps it to grow and develop. Relationships can't survive without it. If your relationship was a car, communication would be the petrol. If your relationship was me, communication would be marshmallows. You need to be able to talk to your partner about your feelings, your worries and insecurities, your needs and desires.

SOME GOOD TIPS FOR COMMUNICATING IN A RELATIONSHIP

1. Be as honest as you can. If you are angry or upset, try to explain why and help your partner understand.

2. Come back to conversations. If you are both upset or angry you won't always be able to sort things out but you can take some time and space to calm down and then revisit the problem.

3. Arranging a time to talk about a particular issue is a good way to make sure you actually discuss it and don't keep chickening out.

4. If you're nervous or emotional about something, you can always write down the key things you want to say and bring them with you, or even send your partner an email first and then meet to discuss it afterwards.

5. Don't try to write important messages on cakes. There's never enough room.

The big thought twist you have to pull off is realizing that your choices come first and the relationship shapes itself around them like a glove – you shouldn't have to be growing fingers (or chopping them off for that matter) to fit somebody else's gauntlet.

This goes for everything from what you like to do at the weekend to what you're ready for in a relationship – you should be deciding together, not feeling pressured to perform to anybody else's pre-decided checklist. And you should always be able to say no, or stop, or I've changed my mind.

Sometimes, we're not the best person to judge how our relationship is going, because, much like being inside a tree trunk, it can be difficult to get perspective from the inside.

YOU CAN

always

This is especially true if things aren't too great, because we tend to think of abuse or relationship violence as something really dramatic that only happens in films and books, not to 'people like me'. We all think 'it can't be me', 'I'm overreacting', 'I'm being over the top'.

But actually it's incredibly common – young people in the UK, the US and many other countries are more likely to experience partner abuse than any other age group. 12.7 per cent of women aged 16–19 have experienced domestic abuse in the last year alone.[1] The NSPCC has found that 33 per cent of girls aged 13–17 have experienced some form of sexual abuse. In the US, young women are three times more likely to experience domestic abuse than any other age group,[2] and 1.5 million high school girls every year experience an incident of physical violence from a dating partner.[3]

It can happen in any kind of relationship, not just a monogamous heterosexual one, and people of any gender can be the victim. In fact, it doesn't happen to one particular 'type' of person – you can be rich or poor, shy or strong, sporty or clever – because it's not about you, it's not your fault or something you did wrong, it's the abusive partner who makes abuse happen. Full stop.

And it doesn't only have to look like hitting or screaming at you either – it could be physical, sexual, emotional, psychological or financial abuse. There are also things that you might not think fit into any of these categories, but still just don't make you feel very good. If that's the case you might want to have a think about the relationship and whether you want to stay in it.

Here are some warning signs you might spot that suggest a relationship isn't very healthy:

- Your partner hurts you physically, including hitting, punching, pinching, scratching, slapping, pushing, burning, beating or pulling hair.

- Your partner pushes you into activities you don't want to do or you're not ready for, including smoking, drinking, taking drugs, kissing, groping your body, genital touching or oral sex, penetrative sex, watching porn or sending sexual images of yourselves.

- Your partner calls you names or says nasty things about you that make you feel scared, sad, hurt, small, embarrassed, intimidated or worthless.

- Your partner puts you down in front of other people.

- Your partner tries to control you, by checking your phone, emails or social media accounts, trying to get you to spend less time with friends or family, telling you you can't talk to certain people, maybe making you feel lonely and cut off.

- They use money to exert control over you, by making you financially dependent on them, restricting your access to money, or buying you things and making you feel pressured to do things in return.

Here are some good signs of a positive relationship:

- You feel loved, safe, respected and free to be yourself.

- You make each other laugh.

- Your partner is pleased for you when you get great news or achieve success.

- You love hanging out together but are also able and happy to spend time apart.

- Your partner stands up for you.

- You support each other through difficult times.

- You take it in turns to make decisions about things like what to do on a date.

- You talk about and equally share bigger decision-making.

- You respect each other's privacy and friendships.

You might spot things from both lists that describe your relationship. That's normal too. But remember that anything from the first list is a cause for concern, and something from the second doesn't cancel it out. Just because your partner says sorry afterwards doesn't make it OK for them to regularly hurt or insult you. Sometimes a partner might say that they did something because they loved you so much, or you made them jealous or angry. None of these are good enough excuses. In fact they're not excuses at all.

A helpful way to think about your relationship a bit more clearly is to ask yourself what you would say to a friend if they were in your shoes. Would you be worried about them? What advice might you give them? We're often more confident and indignant on behalf of the people we love than we are for ourselves, so this can be a good way to get a handle on the situation and work out whether you might need to take action.

If you do think you're in an unhealthy relationship, there is tons of support available to help you. Always put your own safety first. The This Is Abuse website (thisisabuse.direct.gov.uk) has brilliant resources, information, confidential advice and contact details for free. There are more support organizations in the back of the book for different issues too, like abuse that comes from outside a relationship, from a friend, family member or stranger, or particular problems like honour violence, forced marriage or FGM. Help is out there. All you have to do is click the mouse or pick up the phone. You can do it.

Ending relationships can feel sad, scary and awful, but that's not a good enough reason to stay in one if it isn't right. Sometimes the other person is lovely but it just isn't for you any more. Being kind and honest is the best thing you can do for them. Treat them how you'd like to be treated if it were the other way round. Don't tell them there are plenty more fish in the sea or 'it's not you, it's me'! You probably don't need to go into *too* much detail either – they're already being dumped, there's no need to add an exhaustive list of their every flaw. If you're worried, you can always take a friend for moral support.

Being the dumpee isn't much fun either, but I promise you will someday look back and feel OK about it. I was once dumped by a guy who explicitly mentioned, during the dumping explanation, that one of his (many) reasons for breaking up with me was the fact that I couldn't take a sexist joke. At the time, it felt like one of the worst things that had ever happened to me. Now, I feel really, really lucky I didn't end up with the guy who wanted me to stop complaining about sexist jokes and instead I found one who knocks them out of the park.

The way you feel when someone breaks up with you isn't the way you'll feel forever. Knowing that probably won't make you feel much better at the time. But knowing that time will heal things sometimes helps you hang in there.

It's important to know that it will get better. And that when you're feeling down, there are things – real life, ordinary, down-to-earth things – that you can do that might help you feel better. Most of all, remember that no stage of a relationship is likely to be very much like how the movies and the magazines and the YouTube flashmob proposals make it seem. It doesn't just suddenly romantically start pouring with rain but a special kind of rain that doesn't make your mascara run, and makes your hair go stunningly curly instead of leaving you looking like a frizzy hedgehog. You don't usually trip over a tangled dog lead and *whoops* fall right into the arms of Mr or Ms Right. It's not always beautiful and achingly romantic when a relationship ends and you won't always drown your sorrows in a two-litre tub of chocolate-chip ice cream, or sit with your head against a window looking broodingly out at the rain with a glass of red wine, somehow crying beautiful, crystal tears that, again, do not make your mascara run. The truth is it can feel awful. Not just when relationships end, but also when you aren't in one and you feel lonely, or make an advance that's rejected, or feel like nobody will ever fall in love with you. And unlike the movies, most of us don't have quirky hobbies like oil painting that we're so passionate about we can lose our pain in them altogether, or FABULOUS BFFS who distract us with shopping trips where we emerge from changing rooms in cutesy outfits and giggle goofily to a nineties soundtrack and then magically feel better. It can feel really awful. And that's OK. We don't all have Hollywood lives. Not even Hollywood stars have Hollywood lives.

Sometimes, films and TV shows can make it feel like there's something incredibly romantic and quite cool about being in that unhappy place, or being treated badly, but that really *is* an illusion.

Trust yourself. If it feels wrong, it probably is.

And one day you might just find the person who makes you thank your lucky stars it didn't work out before.

CHAPTER EIGHT

IT'S MY FACE AND I'LL SMILE IF I WANT TO

Women are equal to men now. Right?

Spoiler alert: not so much.

When I was growing up I certainly thought they were. I wasn't particularly aware of sexism. If you'd asked me at the age of twenty whether I thought sexism was a major problem, I'd probably have said no. If you'd asked me if I was a feminist, I'd have said 'a what?' If you'd asked me what my favourite TV show was, I'd have said *Neighbours*, but one problem at a time.

To cut a long story short, I left university, moved to London and began to acquire my sexist bullshit klaxon.

What's interesting, though, is that when I look back I can see very clearly that although I hadn't been aware of sexism while I was at school or university, I actually faced it on a regular basis. I just didn't really pick up on it. Sometimes things made me upset and angry, but I didn't know what to call them. I didn't realize they were examples of 'sexism'. I just thought of it as something annoying that was part of life for most girls, like acne or the sticky floor in the H&M changing rooms.

I didn't think it was 'sexism' when boys at school rated the girls out of ten as we came out of the swimming pool changing rooms in our towels, aged about thirteen. But I did remember how confused and embarrassed it made me, how it set us girls up against each other and made us feel like we were supposed to be competing for something. I do remember how it made me feel small.

I didn't think it was 'sexism' when the boys in my GCSE English class taunted me, the only girl in the class, about the 'thunder thighs' of one of my friends until I ran out of the classroom, but I remember how it made my heart race and tears sting the back of my eyes.

I didn't think it was 'sexism' to laugh at girls for not having shaved armpits, or make muttered comments about our bodies and developing breasts, but I know it helped me to understand I was being judged on my figure, and that there were parts of my body I should be ashamed of.

I didn't think it was 'sexism', at university, when my football-playing boyfriend came home from the end of year football dinner with a gold trophy in the shape of a clenched fist with the thumb pointing downwards – the 'under the thumb' award, for the player who'd spent too much time with his girlfriend. I didn't know it was sexism that made the team captain look through me as if I wasn't even there as he berated my boyfriend one evening for going out for a meal with me when the other 'lads' were playing drinking games. But I knew it made me feel invisible, insignificant and inferior.

When men shouted at me in the street, starting when I was about twelve, often in my school uniform, I didn't say anything, because it was scary, and embarrassing. I didn't tell anyone, because I had the vague feeling that it was my fault. And most of all, I never thought of objecting, because I thought it was normal.

It was normal to jump out of my skin when a car beeped its horn unexpectedly as it came up behind me; normal to see the guys inside laughing at me as they sped away; normal to ignore the shouts from building sites; normal to cringe as they turned from 'all right darlin'' to 'fucking slut' when I didn't respond.

And over time it wasn't just the events themselves that became normal, but my reactions to them too.

It became normal to cross the street if I saw a building site ahead; normal to tense up when I saw a lorry or van approaching; normal to pull my skirt down and pull my jacket more closely around me; normal to feel my heart pound and shake as the shouts rained down; normal to feel scared walking in the dark; normal to hold my keys between my fingers just in case; normal to go to the loo in groups; normal to check if my friends were safely home after nights out.

Normal, normal, normal, normal, normal.

As I grew up there were new normals to learn – normal to feel a hand on your side or sliding down to your bum in a club; normal to feel one between your legs at the bar; normal to remove hands from your breasts as you danced; normal to dance back to back with your friends to fend it off; normal to laugh it off, brush it off; normal to be called frigid, or uptight.

Normal to be cornered in a dark deserted street at 11.30 p.m. while two fully grown men laughed to each other, 'We're gonna part those legs and fuck that cunt.'

Normal to have my bottom smacked, hard and without warning, by a stranger in the street. Normal to shrink into my seat in fear and embarrassment when the man across the aisle on the bus began to masturbate, watching me closely.

Normal not to say anything.

Normal to be scared.

Normal.

I never reported a single incident.

It was normal.

According to the dictionary, sexism means prejudice, stereo-typing, or discrimination, typically against women, on the basis of sex. But it's more than that. It's the feeling that you're not quite as good. The suggestion that you're weaker, sillier, secondary, other, lesser. The sense that a public space isn't as much yours as it is a man's. The notion that you have to laugh along at a sexist joke or it's you who's branded uptight, or humourless, not the douchebag making it. The way that 'he' is the automatic default for a person. The fact that insults, from cunt to motherfucker to bastard to pussy, are all, at their root, derogatory towards women. The fact that only seven FTSE 100 companies have female bosses.[1] That women only write one fifth of front page newspaper articles.[2] That they're 50 per cent of chemistry undergraduates but only 6 per cent of professors.[3] That 400,000 women are sexually assaulted in England and Wales every year, and 85,000 raped.[4] The tiny things and the big ones.

I think sexism is a bit like watching a 3D film at the cinema. Once you put on the special glasses, it suddenly jumps out at you, as real as day, in all its technicolour glory, and you can't believe you didn't see it before. Once you put on the glasses, you can't take them off. You see the pieces of naked women in the adverts for gadgets on the tube and wonder how you never realized before that they were using bits of girls to sell products. You start to notice that there's only ever one woman on the TV panel show you love to watch. You hear the ticket collector coming down the train and realize he's calling the men 'sir' and the women 'sweetheart'. You hear a sexist joke and realize how many you've heard before. Your friend says their Facebook account was 'fraped' and you suddenly think about what that means.

In fact, once you start thinking about it, you realize something HUGE. You'd thought you were living in the same world as your guy friends this whole time, but they've had completely different lives . . .

BOYS	GIRLS
Blue hat	Pink hat
'Future Superhero' babygro	'Future Princess' babygro
Trucks and Lego	Toy cookers and dolls
Growing so big and strong!	Getting so pretty!
Bob the Builder and Dr Who	Bratz and Barbie
Knights in shining armour	Damsels in distress
Pirate parties	Fairy parties
Football	Ballet
Muscles	Weight loss
Stud	Slut

And then, because you're seeing it everywhere, you start talking about it. You can't help it. You're seeing this massive phenomenon you've been living in and yet somehow hadn't realized existed, and you want to talk to other people about it too.

But when you talk about sexism, someone tells you it doesn't exist any more.

When you list some of your experiences, they explain you were overreacting, or taking it the wrong way – don't you know he meant it as a compliment?

When they dismiss one incident, it's hard to explain how it feels, how it fits in with all the others.

When a man shouts at you in the street, they say you were asking for it.

When your friend is assaulted, someone asks you what she was wearing.

On the news, a woman is talking about being discriminated against in the workplace. So they have a debate about whether women are making a fuss about nothing.

It's strange, because it's suddenly so real to you, but it doesn't seem like anybody else can see it at all.

Sexism is an invisible problem. It's invisible because we're all so used to it that we don't stop to think about how wrong it is.

So why does it still exist in the twenty-first century? The truth is: *sexism has nothing to do with women.*

The 15 per cent gender pay gap doesn't exist because women are 15 per cent less good at their jobs than men. Parliament and FTSE 100 companies aren't dominated by men because men are just better politicians and businesspeople. Women don't get assaulted and raped because they're 'asking for it'. Even though these are all myths you might have heard.

Sexism exists because it's a power structure – it keeps one half of society held down a little beneath the surface, which makes it easier for the other half to thrive. It's a state of affairs that has developed over the years as multiple factors interact with one another to create a framework that's difficult to challenge, including the fact that women were traditionally expected to stay at home while men went out to work; that women weren't considered capable of playing a part in politics, and weren't even allowed to vote until 1918; that we have rigid expectations of the gendered roles women and men should play and how they should behave in relationships; and that the caring and domestic work largely carried out by women is unpaid and undervalued. The class system and male violence against women have played a role in the development of the power structure too, with women doing the majority of low-paid work and rape within marriage only becoming illegal in England and Wales in 1991.

When a system like this exists, it can be really difficult to dismantle, because it creates an uneven power structure that automatically replicates and reinforces itself. Because the system means that men are far more likely to be in important decision-making roles, the people with the advantage have all the power, and they're not very likely to change the system.

This doesn't mean that all men are evil, or mean, or sexist. The vast majority are not. But the people who benefit from an unequal system often don't tend to notice the problem. They're not incentivized to fix it. It's easy for them to keep drifting on through a world that gives them an automatic head-start without complaining or even noticing.

This doesn't mean that men and boys can't face sexism too. We've all heard of 'man flu', or the idea that 'boys don't cry'. Men experience far higher rates of suicide than women, partly because of damaging stereotypes about having to be tough and 'man up' and not ask for help. But it's also important to realize that, at the broadest, institutional, structural level, sexism disproportionately disadvantages women and girls.

And very often, sexism hurts both men *and* women at the same time. Like the idea that women should stay at home with the kids and men should earn the money – this prevents men from feeling able to spend time with their families *and* holds women back in the workplace. The idea that football is for boys and art is for girls can prevent both girls *and* boys from feeling able to do what they love.

The good news is that addressing sexism is good for everyone. For example, if we solve the problem of women being pressured to take most of the responsibility for childcare, it's great for girls because we won't be seen as a 'risk' by employers and we'd have better opportunities in the workplace. But it'd also be brilliant for men, who would find it easier to battle the stereotypes that might make it harder for them be awarded parental leave, or child custody.

And the *really* good news is, if you're experiencing sexism, or if it really pisses you off, you're not on your own. More and more people are starting to think about gender inequality and starting to stand up to it. There are loads of ways you can get involved (see chapter twelve, 'The F-Word'). And it starts small. It starts with talking to our friends, and calling it out, and knowing our rights.

Here are some real statistics about what girls are putting up with:

- Over a third of teenage girls are put off careers in science because of negative stereotypes[5]
- 43 per cent of young women in London have experienced sexual harassment in public spaces over the past year[6]
- Almost one third of girls experience 'unwanted sexual touching' in UK schools[7]
- 71 per cent of sixteen-year-olds say they hear sexual name calling such as 'slut' and 'slag' used towards girls at school several times a week[8]
- 2,865 sex crimes and 320 rapes were reported in British schools in the past three years[9]

And here are some experiences girls have shared using the #EverydaySexism hashtag on Twitter:

'Getting wolf-whistled twice whilst walking home from school by men more than thirty years older than me'

'Me and my friends got shouted "I'd do all of them" by a group of men in a van as we walked home from school'

'I was thirteen the first time someone shouted "nice tits" at me ... In my school uniform as well ...'

'My school bans girls from wearing short skirts because it'll distract the boys ... why not ban boys from sexualizing girls?'

'I had to switch school because the sexual harassment got so bad'

'Male head of year at my sister's school told girls to "dress appropriately, we don't want 13y/o boys looking at u in THAT way"'

'My school claims we are all equal, yet the P.E. options for boys and girls are different. Boys: table tennis, trampolining, high jump. Girls: dance, aerobics, cheerleading'

'Was told to "move, you stupid little bitch" by man running for train ... I was in school uniform, tying my shoe'

'In my primary school uniform and a man says "I've got a big cock. Want some of it?" I ran across the road and shouted "WANKER"'

'Having my boobs commented on while wearing school uniform and being told it's a compliment'

'When I was thirteen, a man sitting across from me on a crowded train took his penis out and fondled it. No one did anything'

'Rated out of ten and asked if I'm "up for it" by my male class-mates, referred to as "slut" instead of my name'

'"YOU GOT GREAT LEGS IN THAT SCHOOL SKIRT, BABY"'

'Being called a slut at the age of fourteen in my school uniform for not shaving my legs by the boys in my class'

'Age fourteen, walking to school, in uniform, man on a motor-bike reaches out and grabs my breast as he passes me'

'When I was at high school, boys thought it was funny to put their hand between girls' legs as they were climbing the stairs'

'Groped between legs and held down on a school bus age twelve'

'Being followed after school one day and being sexually harassed by some Year Twelves when I WAS twelve "boys will be boys"'

'Having our asses grabbed at school when we were like four-teenish, teachers seeing it and saying nothing'

'In school some of the guys called themselves FBI Federal Breast Inspectors and would grope female students' breasts'

'Being groped daily in primary school aged eleven, headmaster chuckled when I complained. Boys will be boys'

'Chased, groped, and kissed in primary school repeatedly by boy. I said no and I slapped him to get him off. I was punished'

∗

What can you do when something like that happens?

First and most important of all, there's no right answer to this question.

The fact is, these things are awful, they are sexist and they are wrong. However you react, they shouldn't be happening in the first place. There's no 'wrong' thing you did to provoke them and there's no 'right' thing to do when they happen. If you freeze, or panic, that's OK. If you shout back, that's OK. If you report it, that's OK. If you don't feel able to, that's OK. The only person who is at fault here is the person doing the harassing/groping/bullying.

But here are some options that are open to you:

It can be difficult to come up with something to say on the spur of the moment, especially if you're feeling scared or anxious – but if you do want to respond and think it's safe, you can take 'comeback inspiration' from some incredible responses other women and girls have shared with me on Twitter:

'A man just said, whilst staring at my chest, "You look very bountiful this morning." I said, "Yes, I'm about to menstruate"'

'Guy makes orgasm noise at me as I walk past. Me: "That will probably be the only time you ever hear that noise in your life"'

'Random man on street: "fat cow". Me: "I can lose weight, you'll always be a wanker"'

'A man once pointed out loudly that I have huge boobs. I looked down at them and screamed like I'd never noticed them before'

'In response to an older guy asking "where have you been all my life?"; "An unfertilized egg in my mother's ovary, you creep"'

'A friend heard a guy shout, "Sit on my face!" at a girl who replied, "Why, is your nose bigger than your dick?" AMAZING!'

'Had a guy say "Your cleavage!" My response: "You single?" Him: "Yeah!!" Me: "I can see why"'

Alternatively, some fantastic anti-street harassment organizations suggest this simple trick:

- Describe the culprit
- Describe the behaviour

E.g. 'Man in the grey T-shirt, stop stroking my legs.'

This takes all the shame and embarrassment that we sometimes (unfairly) feel when someone harasses us, and puts it firmly on the shoulders of the harasser. It also sends a clear signal to passers-by: lets them know there's a problem and gives them a chance to step in and help you.

But remember, the easiest time to respond to sexual harassment or sexism is when you're not actually the target. Being an active bystander means not looking the other way or pretending it's normal or acceptable, but raising your voice if it feels safe to do so. If we all did this, we'd send the most incredibly powerful message to sexists and harassers.

And at school or university, this means having other girls' backs by not laughing along or ignoring sexism and harassment. It also means calling guys out on it and supporting each other to report it together if you feel able to. The more people who come forward, the more pressure on the institution to deal with the problem.

Your school, college or university has a pastoral duty to protect you from harassment and discrimination and they should damn well be living up to it – don't be afraid to report to them and demand they take action.

Outside school or university, there are other options. One woman who wrote to me said a man working on a roof shouted about her breasts as she walked past, so she stopped and told him how upset it made her feel and how rude he was being. He ignored her and shouted more, so she carefully moved away the ladder leading up to the roof and walked away, leaving him stuck up there to think about what he'd done. But if you don't happen to have the time or the energy for that, reporting someone who harasses you from a van or on a construction site directly to their company is another great way to make sure they get the message.

You know that story about how a pregnant woman is legally allowed to pee in any policeman's helmet? Well, you might be surprised about some other services the police have a duty to provide too. We get so used to putting up with this crap that it can feel too petty or trivial, and you might worry about not being taken seriously. That's completely understandable. But you'd be surprised how much you *do* have the right to report, if you want to . . .

KNOW YOUR RIGHTS

- The **Protection From Harassment Act 1997** makes it an offence for someone to engage in a course of conduct which they know or ought to know is harassing, alarming or distressing someone

- The **Public Order Act 1986** makes it an offence for someone to cause intentional harassment, alarm or distress including by using threatening, abusive or insulting words or behaviour, or disorderly behaviour

Sexist, unwanted and aggressive behaviour like obscene comments and catcalls, being followed or persistently harassed may all fall under these two categories

- The **Sexual Offences Act 2003** makes it an offence for someone to intentionally expose their genitals with the intention of causing another person alarm or distress

This covers anybody who deliberately flashes you or masturbates in front of you

- The **Sexual Offences Act 2003** sets out the legal definition of sexual assault:

A person (A) commits an offence if:

(a) They intentionally touch another person (B),
(b) The touching is sexual,
(c) B does not consent to the touching, and
(d) A does not reasonably believe that B consents.

This could include somebody groping, touching, stroking, grabbing, poking, caressing, licking or kissing you on your legs, thighs, bottom, crotch, stomach, breasts or elsewhere.

As you can see, the law protects girls from a LOT of things that we often just put up with as 'part of life'.

Let's stop for a moment to really recognize that a lot of what girls are putting up with on a regular basis, in school and out, is defined as <u>sexual assault</u> under UK law.

It shouldn't be this way. This behaviour is illegal and you can report it.

Reporting to the police doesn't mean you will have to press charges or go to court – you can always choose to stop at any stage in the process. If you don't feel able to report, that's also OK. There are lots of women, and in particular certain groups, including women of colour, sex workers and LGBT* folk, who don't always feel safe turning to the police for help because of ingrained patterns of racist, homophobic, transphobic or stigmatizing behaviour within law enforcement. It's not your responsibility to report unless you feel that you can. But sometimes it can help give you a sense of closure or control.

Sometimes, though, it can feel like the trickiest incidents to deal with are the most 'minor'. Like the put-down that's disguised as 'banter'. The sexist 'joke'. The muttered comment you don't quite catch. The 'compliment' that's screamed at you in the street.

Just to be clear, here's a helpful graph for boys who might be considering taking up the great tradition of shouting at women they don't know in the street:

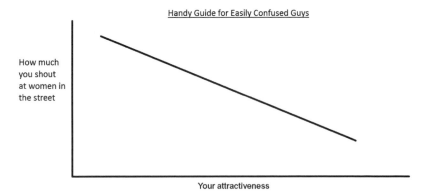

Handy Guide for Easily Confused Guys

How much you shout at women in the street

Your attractiveness

This mysterious confusion between harassment and flirting has been handed down for many centuries, as this ancient Roman limerick clearly demonstrates:

> There once was a Roman spear carrier
> Seeing a woman, he started to harry her
> He whistled and groped her
> Then looked up her toga
> So clearly she begged him to marry her
> NOT.

The thing about catcalling is that all the arguments in its favour are deeply, deeply flawed, which makes you kind of suspicious. Here are some of the ways people defend catcalling:

1. It's harmless
2. It's a compliment
3. It's flirting – can't men ever approach women now?
4. Girls wouldn't dress like that if they didn't want attention
5. Why make a fuss about a wolf-whistle when there are bigger problems like rape?

The problem is, none of it stands up to scrutiny.

1. If it was harmless, there wouldn't be hundreds of articles written about it, regular debates on radio and television and thousands of women tweeting, writing and arguing that it makes them feel crap/scared/embarrassed/angry/objectified.

2. I think we can all agree that a compliment is intended to make someone feel good about themselves. But for many women this is clearly not the impact of having someone

shouting about their 'snatch' in the street. And the idea of it being a compliment is kind of undermined by the number of women who try to ignore or reject it only to find that it changes and becomes aggressive, threatening and abusive. 'All right, darling' turns quick as a flash into 'Fuck you, slag' when you reject the advance, which doesn't seem very complimentary to me. (Or very logical – how does saying *no* to a sexual advance make you a slag?)

3. No. Woman. Ever. Has chased after a man who shouted about her tits out of his car window, begging him to stop and marry her. So the argument that this is a form of flirting really doesn't make a lot of sense. Have you ever met a couple who got together because he screamed a comment about her fine arse across the street at a busy traffic junction? Me neither. Plus, this is really insulting to the vast majority of lovely guys who know perfectly well how to tell the difference between harassment and flirting . . .

FLIRTING Vs. HARASSMENT

4. What we wear isn't about you. Shocker.

5. The weird non-argument that you can't make a fuss about something because it isn't as serious as something else doesn't get used in other debates, and is just a way of trying to shut women up. We have every right to fight back against street harassment because

a) It does matter – it can have a huge impact, happen regularly and seriously impact women's lives, so it is a big deal

b) We can tackle this and also other problems like domestic violence *at the same time*

c) Any form of harassment and inequality is worth speaking out about

d) The 'smaller things' like street harassment all add up and help contribute to the kind of attitudes towards women that enable the bigger things to happen. If we say it's OK to treat women like second-class citizens in the street, how can we demand they're respected in the workplace? If we say women's bodies are public property in public spaces, it's harder to argue they deserve complete control over them in the bedroom. And so on.

If you're coming up against a lot of 'minor' sexism, you might need to build yourself a Bullshit Detection Kit.

Ask yourself these simple questions:

- Is the same thing happening to my male peers?
- Have I been told to calm down and not make a fuss about it?
- Does it *feel* like bullshit?

If the answer to one or more of the above questions is yes, there's a strong possibility you've got a case of bullshit on your hands (*no one* likes having bullshit on their hands).

If you do find yourself coming across a case of sexism, you're going to need an action plan.

ACTION PLAN FOR CHALLENGING SEXIST BULLSHIT

1. Be specific

You don't have to call someone 'a sexist' – they'll probably react defensively and try and argue back if you do. What sometimes has better results is to lay out exactly what the problem is and how it affected you. For example, 'When you said this, it made me feel like that.'

2. Pick your moment

Confronting someone in a big group might work but it might also make them feel defensive and more likely to react angrily or aggressively. Sometimes a quiet word somewhere not too busy is the best way to give a person the chance to reflect on what they've done.

3. Don't be defeated

If your initial plan doesn't work, or if things get worse, you can always try another method. If you try to deal with things yourself first and that doesn't work, you could progress to reporting the problem. (Also, don't feel defeated if somebody doesn't immediately drop on their knees before you and repent their sexist ways. It's pretty hard for any of us to admit we were wrong when we're called out on it, but even if somebody reacts defensively in the moment you might still have made them go away and think about it later.)

4. Stick together

It can be much easier to call this stuff out as a team than on your own. It makes it less scary, it makes you less likely to deal with nastiness afterwards, and it makes it harder for the culprit to argue back. Check out the 'F-Word' chapter for some great ways for young women to take action together.

If guys you know are often sexist, coming together as a group with other girls to challenge them on it can be really effective.

Part of sticking together and having each other's backs is being aware that sexism also affects different people in different ways, as is quite well summed up by this headline that popped up on my computer today: 'Seventeen celebrity lesbians you will definitely fancy'.

I mean, literally, what? Sometimes headline writers just need to get in the sea.

Unfortunately, the narrow-minded prejudice of sexism often goes hand-in-hand with other types of narrow-minded prejudice, including racism, homophobia, transphobia, ableism, ageism, classism and stigma against groups like sex workers, larger people, or people with mental health problems. If we're going to fight sexism, we have to be prepared to stand up against other inequalities as well. This might mean educating yourself about issues your friends and peers face in combination with sexism that you might not deal with yourself.

And finally, for dealing with those *hilarious* cracks about women and the kitchen:

FIVE WAYS TO DEAL WITH A SEXIST JOKE

1. In a very pleasant tone, with a slightly mystified smile, as if you just didn't quite catch the punchline, ask the person to explain the joke. Then watch as they make themselves sound stupider and stupider and get more and more flustered trying to explain the sexist joke. At no point step in and release the tension. Keep asking them to be more specific.

2. Place an entire large, smushy food item (a banana or a doughnut would work splendidly here) in your mouth, chew a couple of times, and then very deliberately smile widely at them.

3. Tell them, 'The 1950s called . . . they want their punchline back.'

4. Say, 'Haha, I see, it's funny because . . .' and then add the sexist premise. Like 'Haha, I see, it's funny because women can't drive'. Then give them your best side-eye.

5. Say 'OMG, that's hilarious, would it still be so funny if someone was saying it about your mum/sister/girlfriend?'

Overall, remember 'it's my x and I'll y if I want to' is an excellent rule of thumb.

It's my face and I'll smile if I want to.

It's my body and I'll shave if I want to.

It's my vagina and I'll masturbate if I want to.

It's my ~~mop~~ broomstick and I'll pretend to be Hermione Granger if I want to.

Stop judging me.

But it is pretty tough for guys with all these confusing decisions to make. After all, they are overwhelmed with options and it can be difficult to work out what is and isn't sexist, right? Just try putting yourself in their shoes ... and choose your own adventure.

1. At an evening event you see a woman you find attractive. Do you:

  a) Approach politely and strike up a conversation [go to 2]

  b) Grab her bum [go to 10]

  c) Shout 'TITS' across the crowded room and wait eagerly for her to run into your arms [go to 11]

2. She tells you her name and you try to think of what to say next. Do you:

  a) Try and get to know her by asking about her hobbies and interests [go to 3]

  b) Tell her: 'Nice dress! It'd look better on my bedroom floor' [go to 12]

  c) Get her talking and grab her boob at the earliest opportunity [go to 10]

3. After a short chat, you move onto the dance floor. Do you:
  a) Have fun dancing with her [go to 4]
  b) Immediately try to grab her bum [go to 10]
  c) Pour your drink over her and shout 'WET T-SHIRT COMPETITION, BRO' (there is no wet T-shirt competition) [go to 13]

4. The end of the night approaches and you want to suggest taking things to the next level. Do you:
  a) Communicate this by grabbing her boob [go to 10]
  b) Ask her 'Do you like Harry Potter? Because I want to Slyther-in ya' [go to 6]
  c) Ask if she'd be interested in coming back to your place [go to 5]

5. She explains that, although she has had a good time, she doesn't feel like taking things any further tonight. Do you:
  a) Totally respect her decision and exchange numbers before you leave [go to 7]
  b) Laugh in her face, call her a fucking slut and say you weren't interested anyway [go to 13]
  c) Pressure and cajole her, refuse to take no for an answer and basically physically carry her into a cab [go to 9]
  d) Grab her boob [go to 10]

6. She replies: 'You have five seconds to step back before I stick my Ravenclaws into you.' Do you:
  a) Apologize and back off [go to 7]
  b) Grab her boob [go to 10]
  c) Throw caution to the wind and shout 'TITS!' [go to 11]

7. As you wave her off into the distance and turn to go home, you feel a tap on your shoulder. You turn to see a startlingly beautiful girl you hadn't noticed before. She says your simple human decency and respectful behaviour towards her friend have massively turned her on. She leans in for the kiss ... You end up back at her place and the sex is fucking awesome because she actually really wanted to have sex with you [go to 8]

8. NOT! You don't get a cookie just for clearing the low bar of being a decent human being. What, do you think women owe you sex just for not being a total arsehole? Jeez! But you did make it through the evening without being a total jackass or committing a felony: MAZEL TOV! You didn't ruin your chances with the first woman by being a dickbag so there's every chance she might want to see you again. THE END.

9. You get back to your place and realize she's actually pretty drunk. Do you:
   a) Tuck her up in your bed, making sure she's in the recovery position, and check on her regularly through the night to make sure she hasn't been sick [go to 14]
   b) Think this seems like a great time to have sex, even though she's not really responding [go to 15]
   c) Wait until she passes out then have sex with her [go to 16]
   d) Ask her if she wants to have sex and interpret her drunkenness as a yes [go to 17]
   e) Presume it's cool to have sex since she kissed you a lot earlier, even though she's not doing much now [go to 18]

  f) Assume it's cool to have sex because she has taken
   some of her clothes off, even though she doesn't seem
   that into it [go to 19]

  g) Assume you can have sex even though she's out of it
   because she's got you turned on now, so she's got to
   go through with it [go to 20]

  h) Try to wake her up by shouting 'TITS!' [go to 11]

10. She empties her drink over your head and hands you a
laminated copy of Part 1 Section 3 of the Sexual Offences
Act 2003. You realize you've just committed a sexual
assault, punishable by imprisonment. You go home, dry
your hair, watch *The Notebook* and re-evaluate your life
choices. THE END.

11. You see a flash of bright colour out of the corner of your
eye and hear a strange whooshing sound. Suddenly you're
surrounded by a twittering flock of small blue and yellow
birds. They start pecking at your clothes, your face, your
eyes. 'MY EYES!' you shriek, realizing that you can no
longer see. And that's why you should *never* shout tits.
THE END.

12. She replies, 'Nice suit, it'd look better on someone who
isn't a jackass' and walks away. Commiserations. *Unless
this is totally the reaction you were going for, in which
case CONGRATULATIONS!* THE END.

13. She looks at you for a beat, then goes over to the bar,
pulls out the soda hose and sprays you with it for five
minutes while all the women in the room cheer. You have

to move to a different town because none of the women you live near will speak to you any longer. THE END.

14. Later the next day, you feel a tap on your shoulder. You turn to see a startlingly beautiful girl you hadn't noticed before. She says your simple human decency and respectful behaviour towards her friend last night have massively turned her on. She leans in for the kiss ... You end up back at her place and the sex is fucking awesome because she actually really wanted to have sex with you [go to 8]

15. You're a rapist. THE END.

16. You're a rapist. THE END.

17. You're a rapist. THE END.

18. You're a rapist. THE END.

19. You're a rapist. THE END.

20. You're a rapist. THE END.

Huh. Maybe it's not that complicated after all.

CHAPTER NINE

CLITORISH ALLSORTS

They say you never forget your first time
They say the first time is always a disappointment
They say the fifth time's a charm
They say you have to kiss a lot of frogs to find your prince
They say you need to lose your V plates
They say you'll always be glad you waited for the right person
to come along

This is why it's extremely inadvisable to take anything 'they' say too seriously. Who are 'they' anyway, and why do they keep contradicting themselves?

The truth is, no one general rule can tell you how you should feel and what choices you should make about sex. Like the longstanding and equally serious debate about how to eat your creme egg, you have to ignore the propaganda and go with your gut. There's nothing embarrassing about having sex for the first time in your twenties, or your thirties, or your eighties, or not at all, if that's when it's right for you.

I'm not here to tell you what to do. You get enough of that already. I just want you to know you have options. And if it feels like you don't, that might be a sign that something's wrong.

It might help you to work out what 'right for you' looks like if we talked about sex. But in the UK, we seem to be terrified that even whispering the word *sex* is likely to send impressionable, hormone-ridden teenagers into a humping frenzy. As if they had never considered it before and will be unable to control themselves once the topic has arisen.

Amongst our peers, we can sometimes talk about sex a bit more, but even there, there is this idea that the way we talk about it has to be gendered. Guys can talk about sex more openly, but only in a braggy, knowing kind of way, and they're pressured to boast about it, whereas girls who talk about it openly risk being called slags. Amongst themselves, maybe girls feel more able to discuss it than guys, but that's not much help if you're all asking the same questions and nobody has many answers. (My teenage girlfriends and I spent hours debating whether it was true that you get stuck together if you have sex in the bath. Not true, FYI, though you might end up getting the bubbles in some interesting places.)

Personally, I feel like you can be trusted not to start uncontrollably orgasming all over the place if we merely discuss sex, so here are answers to all the questions I wished someone could have answered for me as a teenager. (NB If you do start irrepressibly coming everywhere after reading this chapter, please let me know so I can patent it.)

You can enjoy sex in lots of different ways, at different places and times, and for different reasons. We often talk about sex as if it is one very specific thing, enjoyed in exactly the same way (the 'right' way) by everybody. We talk about it as if the first time is a huge deal that you have to get right or wrong, and that if you wait too long, or not long enough, do it in the wrong way, or the wrong place, or with the wrong person, you will find yourself somehow shamefully declared a failure by a shadowy, universal and all-powerful sex judge.

This is silly.

There are few other activities that we treat in this way, as if the first time we do it is somehow much more important than all the others. Nobody is freaking out about exactly when and how you 'pop' your ice-skating cherry, for example. Come to mention it, isn't there something suspiciously sexist about the idea of 'cherry popping' in the first place? This is not something we are hearing associated with men. We seem to be very much less concerned with men's 'first times' than with women's. We are not universally losing our shit over a random, unimportant, irrelevant membrane that may or may not partially cover an opening in a *man's* body.

The hymen, for the record, is a thin tissue found just inside the vaginal opening. It is gradually worn away over time by factors like hormones, vaginal discharge, tampon use and physical activity. Contrary to popular belief, the hymen does not completely cover the vaginal opening and it does not necessarily 'pop' or 'break' the first time you have sex – it may well already have worn away by then. It is possible that there may be a little bleeding the first time you have sex. The hymen is *not* a handy, button-on-the-top-of-the-jam-jar style indicator of whether or not the seal has been tampered with and this item should be returned to Asda. It's also archaic to think that a person's value should be based on whether or not they have had sex before. What a weird concept. It's even weirder if we arbitrarily make this judgement about girls but not about guys. Again, I call bullshit.

I blame those fussy-eating dragons from olden times who'd demand twenty virgins a year be brought to them in return for not burning down the village. Why not pick a more relevant thing for these young women not to have done – 'bring me twenty girls who have never done any weight-lifting so will be nice and tender' or 'bring me women who have only eaten garlic for the last year'? A virgin and a non-virgin surely taste pretty much exactly the same, no? So what's the big deal?

It's only girls' virginity that gets discussed as if it's this precious, priceless white flower that gets plucked at the opportune moment. Just think about language for a second. It's all framed in terms of guys taking something from girls. We talk about 'giving it away' or 'putting out'. We talk about 'saving' our virginity '*for*' someone special.

Virginity is one of those things that sounds like a huge deal because we talk about it ALL THE TIME but it kind of doesn't really exist – like the Easter bunny, or Russell Brand's personality.

There's nothing wrong or different about you after you have sex! We've made it up!

But how will you know when you're ready to have sex? It's probably one of the most popular questions of all time. Generally, the answer probably is that if you're asking the question, you might not be ready yet. Often, when you're ready, you'll know. If you're not sure, you may as well wait until you are. There's no good reason to rush having sex for the first time – in fact, any reason that you're feeling rushed could be a sign it's not right.

It's a good idea to take your own temperature (metaphorically, not literally, though come to mention it, you probably shouldn't have sex if you have a fever either). Are you feeling relaxed, safe, excited? Are you absolutely sure your partner is as comfortable and enthusiastic as you are? Do you feel like you and your partner really care about each other? Have you talked about contraception and sexual health and made a decision about how to take care of these things together? If the answer to all these is yes, then you might well be ready to go. But do you feel anxious, worried, upset or at all pressured? Do you go back and forth about whether you want to do it or not? Do you think you might regret it or feel bad afterwards? Do you feel like you're doing it because your partner wants to, not you? Are you worried about losing your partner if you don't do it? Are you doing it because other people are? If the answer to any of these is yes, then you might not be ready yet. There is absolutely, completely, utterly ZERO shame in not being ready yet. Deciding you're not quite ready is actually one of the most powerful and mature decisions you'll ever make. It's putting you and your own needs first. Anyone who makes you feel like you have to do it or you'll lose them probably doesn't deserve to do it with you in the first place. And anyone who makes you feel bad by going on and on about their own sexual exploits may well be exaggerating because they feel insecure – this is SO common there's even a word for it: a pornocchio!

In some situations, you might want to use the 'does a person who [insert how they treat you here] deserve to have sex with me?' test.

It pretty much does what it says on the tin.

Example:

Does a person who is trying to push me into it when I've already told him I don't feel ready deserve to have sex with me?

Probably not.

Does a person who hasn't bothered to talk it through with me and check in about how I'm feeling deserve to have sex with me?

No.

Does a person . . .

No, no, he doesn't.

Does a . . .

Again, no.

Does . . .

Same answer.

Yeah . . . NO.

Uh-uh.

Nooope.

Nada.

Nah-uh.

Nopity nopity nope.

Absolument pas.

Of course, once you've got that test down, there's a second test, which is even more important, because someone treating you well doesn't give them any automatic *right* to sex with you. This one's pretty simple too. It goes like this:

'Do I really *want* to have sex with this person?'

Remember, when you do decide it's the right time, you also don't have to go straight from 0 to 100mph. You're not Lewis

Hamilton. It makes sense to take things one step at a time – from kissing to touching to anything else you want to try – you don't have to do it all in one go.

It is also important to know that in the UK the legal age of consent is sixteen. That means that having sex, including oral sex or masturbating together, with anyone under the age of sixteen is illegal, for people of any genders, even with consent. (And from sixteen to eighteen, it's illegal for anyone in a position of care, like a teacher or doctor to have sex with you.)

But beyond that, the time, the place, the type, the partners, the frequency, the positions, the costumes, the props, the foodstuffs are *all* up to you!

In fact, sex is a lot like ice cream (go with me here).

It comes in an almost infinite number of different flavours, even though people often automatically assume you're talking about vanilla, strawberry or chocolate. When we talk about sex, people often assume it's heterosexual, two-person, missionary, in-bed sex, for no good reason at all.

Some people like to try lots of different flavours and others like to have the same flavour over and over again. Just like some people like a variety of partners or positions, roles or kinks. There's absolutely nothing wrong with people liking any flavour of ice cream, even if it is a little out of the ordinary, or isn't to your own personal taste. (The metaphor breaks down here, because people who like pistachio ice cream are sick and wrong and must be stopped, whereas there's nothing wrong with enjoying any kind of sex as long as it's consensual.)

Some people like sprinkles, or nuts, caramel sauce or other toppings with their ice cream. Some people like to have sex using sex toys or ropes or role play ... Or sprinkles, nuts and caramel sauce, come to think of it.

Some folk just don't enjoy it and people often act like that's weird, but actually this is much more common than you might think (with both sex and ice cream).

What's most important of all is that you'd never force-feed ice cream to somebody who said they didn't want any. What a weird thing to do. People eat ice cream because they enjoy it, or it makes them feel good, or it's a pleasurable thing to enjoy on their own or with somebody they're close to. Nobody experiences any of these feelings from being force-fed ice cream when they don't feel like it. You'd never turn up at someone's house and prise a spoon between their lips unexpectedly without offering them ice cream first. Even if you came over planning to have ice cream, if they didn't want any you'd put it away again. It doesn't stop you from going off and having some ice cream on your own, but you can't force them to have any if they don't feel like it. Even if someone initially thought they felt like ice cream, and got out the bowls and spoons, it is still completely their right to decide if they change their mind and don't want any after all. They equally have every right to push the bowl away in the middle of a scoop if they've had enough, or decide they want to stop eating it. If someone has decided they want one particular flavour of ice cream, you wouldn't suddenly shove a different kind in their mouth while they're in the middle of eating it. If they were asleep, or unconscious, or very drunk, you wouldn't just randomly start feeding it to them. And having ice cream with someone once doesn't give you the right to just assume they'll always want to split a sundae with you in the future.

All these things also apply to sexual consent.*

Some people like their ice cream in a cone and some people like

*There are other great analogies to explain consent online – check out Alli Kirkham's consent comics on Everyday Feminism and Emmeline May's fab video about tea on the RockstarDinosaurPiratePrincess blog.

it with those little plastic coloured spoons ... OK, the comparison has its limits. But you see my point.

There's a lot of confusion about sexual consent and what it means. But it's actually pretty simple. It's important to know that any sex without consent is rape (including oral sex, manual sex, or using other objects). In other words, there's actually no such thing as sex without consent – because it would have to be described as rape. (This is a distinction the newspapers aren't always very good at making, which is partly why there is so much widespread misunderstanding about it.)

What this means is that a rapist is not just a stranger in a dark alleyway. A rapist is a boy who pushes his girlfriend into having sex when she isn't ready. A rapist is someone who insists when their partner isn't sure. A rapist is someone who keeps going when you say no, or when you're clearly unhappy. Or when you're unresponsive and obviously not into it.

If you want to have sex with someone else then you have to make absolutely sure that they want to first, and keep on being sure that they want to all the way through. And that doesn't just apply to penis-in-vagina sex, but any kind of sexual activity between any people.

The odd thing is that a lot of people seem to have a problem with this. People say it's over the top, or it's going to ruin all sexual excitement because you have to get some kind of formal agreement signed. I don't think those people have had much sex. First of all, you don't need a signed contract to know that somebody is having a good time and wants to carry on – they often show it with sounds and actions, like kissing and touching you, murmuring or saying they like what you're doing, and reciprocating. And the thing is, if you aren't sure, it's really not that hard to check. It hardly has to mean whipping out a fountain pen and a fifty-seven page legal document.

Sex

WITHOUT

CONSENT

is

RAPE

NOBODY

HAS *any* RIGHT
TO TOUCH YOU
without YOUR
CONSENT

Alongside consent, the one other completely essential ingredient for sex is communication. It's as essential to sex as it is to relationships. You just can't make really great sex without it. It would be like trying to make pancakes without eggs. Like music without Beyoncé. Like apple juice without chips. (Just me?)

The best way to be confident that your partner consents is to communicate. Not just in the heat of the moment, but beforehand, during and afterwards. After all, you don't just want to know that someone's ready to go ahead, you want to be sure that they're just as bouncing-off-the-wall, dancing-on-the-ceiling, can-hardly-contain-themselves ecstatic about getting jiggy with it as you are.

With all this talk about consent, it's easy to think that just 'giving in' or being prepared to go through with it is the key green-light moment for sex. But actually it's the bare minimum. One mum of a college student wrote on Twitter about the best piece of sex advice her son had been given at his college orientation. This is what she shared:

'Consent is really too low a bar. Hold out for enthusiasm.'

There are also lots of other reasons why communication is important for good sex. It helps you to feel more closely connected to your partner, which can make a huge difference to how good the sex feels. It allows you to let your partner know what feels good, what you like, what you want more of etc.

And letting your partner know what feels good to you is important. When I Googled 'Top ten ways to please your ...', the top three search hits were 'man', 'husband' and 'man in bed'. We live in a world where sex is often presented as something primarily for male pleasure, which is really stupid when you consider what a cooperative activity it is. So use your words, and your mmms and aahs, because everybody, not just men, deserves to get the maximum pleasure from sex.

Talking of talking, the words we use to talk about sex matter a lot. You might notice that I haven't used the words 'naughty' or 'dirty' in this book. That's because, although they've taken on the meaning 'sexy', they come from the idea that sex is a bit bad, or wrong, or disgusting, which is just stupid. Another subtly judgemental term we use when we talk about sex is to say someone (usually female) is 'asking for it', or 'gagging for it'. This can be used to victim-blame sexual assault victims, but it can also just be used to describe a girl who seems to be up for sex, or who enjoys and initiates sex.

Why does 'asking for it' have to be a bad thing anyway? There are loads of things girls often don't ask for because we don't want to seem needy, greedy, or boastful. These include:

Asking for a promotion
Asking for extra help
Asking for love
Asking for space
Asking for seconds
Asking for an explanation
Asking for honesty
Asking for a pay rise
Asking for answers
Asking for a re-mark
Asking for a second chance
Asking for support
Asking for more
Asking for cake

The idea that we shouldn't be asking for things comes from outdated sexist notions about sweet, innocent, undemanding women who only get what they're given and wait until a strong, protective man is so generous as to select it for them and drop it in their lap.

" CONSENT *is really too* LOW *a bar*

HOLD OUT

for

ENTHUSIASM

"

If you've been taught that women don't enjoy or direct sex, that it's something that happens to you when you reluctantly let your guard down and decide to put up with it, then try to wipe all that total rubbish out of your brain right now.

There's also this idea that you should only ever have sex if it's 'meaningful', or you're deeply in love. While many people feel this, especially for their first time, there's also nothing wrong with enjoying sex for its own sake. Nobody seems to have a problem with guys doing this but with girls it's often seen as 'slutty' or bad.

This is total bollocks. You can enjoy a healthy and pleasurable sex life just as much as the next person of any gender. There is nothing wrong with enjoying and initiating sex, whatever your gender.

And speaking of bollocks, it's also worth learning a few sexual terms so you don't feel out of the loop if they come up (pun intended). For example, if a guy asks you for a hand-job, he's probably asking you to take his penis in your hand and move it up and down until he ejaculates. If he asks for a sixty-nine, he's probably talking about positioning yourselves so you can each give the other oral sex simultaneously. And if he tries to come on your face, he's probably a dickhead. (Unless it's something you've mutually agreed on as something you want to try – some people enjoy it consensually. But there's a hell of a difference between the two.)

There was a girl at my school who spent months completely mortified because it somehow became public knowledge that she assumed a blow job involved delicately blowing on a guy's penis the way you would on a hot portion of chicken and mushroom soup. And why not? In her defence, that is totally what it sounds like. Luckily for her, after a couple of months another girl accidentally put two tampons in at the same time by mistake and everybody forgot all about the blow job thing. But still, it can be helpful to know what people mean when they use certain terms, so with that in mind, here's a brief glossary of words and their sexplanations (sorry, couldn't resist) that might be useful:

TO HAVE SEX: bang, fuck, bone, boink, get laid, boff, shag, pork, poke, bonk, screw, bump, hump, bump uglies, doink, do, duke, get lucky, get it on, get some, give it up, give it to, put out, go all the way, hit it, kertang, pound, plow, pile, pipe, nail, make whoopee, rail, ram, ride, root, score, slap and tickle, make the beast with two backs, know in the biblical sense, pull ass, push rope, hide the salami, ride the flagpole, seal the deal, slay, sleep with, smash, smack, smush, spank, squeak, stang, swack, tap

KISSING WITH TONGUES: French kissing, tonsil tennis. (Public service announcement: a windmill/washing machine motion is not necessary. You're kissing, not carrying out a 360-degree archaeological excavation. You know who you are)

AN ERECTION OF THE PENIS: boner, hard-on, stiffy, wood, woody

TESTICLES/ SCROTUM: balls, ballsack, bollocks, family jewels

THE SOUND THAT'S MADE BY AIR BEING EXPELLED FROM THE VAGINAL OPENING, SOMETIMES DURING OR AFTER SEX, SOMETIMES CAUSED BY CHANGING POSITIONS DURING INTERCOURSE AS AIR BECOMES TRAPPED IN THE VAGINA*: queef, fanny fart, muff puff

LICKING THE AREA AROUND OR IN YOUR PARTNER'S ANUS: rimming, rim job, anilingus

RUBBING YOUR GENITALS UP AGAINST SOMEONE ELSE'S: dry humping, frotting, frottage. (Get permission first. You are not a Labrador)

TO ORGASM: come, cum, blow your load, hit the big O, get off, finish

SEMEN: come, cum, cream, jizz, gizm, baby gravy, cupid's toothpaste, spooge

CONDOM: johnnie, rubber, French tickler, love glove

MANUALLY STIMULATING A VULVA/VAGINA: finger, fingering, finger fucking (involves touching and stroking around the clitoris, vulva and vagina or inserting one or more fingers into the vagina)

MANUALLY STIMULATING A PENIS: giving a hand-job, tossing off, polishing the knob (involves stroking and touching the penis, often in an up and down motion with the hand around it)

---

* Ways to deal with a fanny fart: 1) Laugh about it – your partner will follow your lead 2) Explain that this is a common by-product of great sex and your partner should consider themselves lucky 3) Use it to blow up a small balloon and distract your partner by making them a model of a poodle.

TO MASTURBATE: wank, Barclays Bank, bash the bishop, jerk off, jack off, toss off, flick the bean

GIVING ORAL SEX TO SOMEONE WITH A VAGINA: cunnilingus, licking out, carpet munching, muff diving, going down on (involves licking or kissing in and around the vagina, clitoris, and vulva)

GIVING ORAL SEX TO SOMEONE WITH A PENIS: giving a blow job, giving head, sucking off, going down on (involves licking or gently sucking the penis, often taking it inside the mouth with an up and down motion)

ANAL SEX: bum sex, backdoor sex, butt love, bone-smuggling, ploughing the back field, uphill gardening, Greek sex (NB: some of these terms have had historical homophobic/criminalization connotations or might be pejorative)

I'm not listing all these because you *need* to know what they all are, or should ever feel *any* pressure to engage in any of them, except those you want to. But knowing what people are talking about can make you feel more confident and in control.

Most importantly, there is no sex God arbiter of the 'right' sex or the 'best' sex, a) because that would be really weird and frankly quite voyeuristic and b) because there is no such thing as the 'best' sex, only the best sex for you, and even that won't be the same on Tuesday afternoon as it is on Saturday night, or with one partner as it is with another, or after a big meal as it is in the middle of your period or ... you get the idea.

It's completely normal for people who have vaginas not to orgasm every time they have sex – in fact, it's actually relatively rare for women to regularly orgasm from vaginal penetration alone (only 25 per cent do).[1] This is because most people need clitoral stimulation as well. This can sometimes be achieved by certain sex positions that stimulate the clitoris, but it's also just as pleasurable for either partner to stimulate the clitoris with their fingers during sex. (Or during masturbation!) Don't ever be afraid to talk to your partner, tell them what feels good and what doesn't and ask for what you want them to do. We're so used to the idea that sex either happens silently or is directed towards male pleasure that it can feel scary to focus on your own pleasure and to ask for it. But your partner is probably hugely keen to make you feel good – they'll be glad to know exactly what you want. Sex should be great for everyone involved – it's not just about pleasing your partner, it's about your enjoyment too!

There are also a million reasons why one or more partners might not always come from sex and it often has nothing to do with how good the sex was – it might be because you're worried or stressed, distracted, or it might be for no rhyme or reason. This is totally normal. The end goal of sex doesn't have to be orgasm every time – it's just unrealistic to think like that and also silly, because the other aspects of sex can feel amazing too.

So you shouldn't panic, or feel like you've got it wrong if you don't think you've had an orgasm.

If you're wondering 'what is an orgasm?' that's a very good question! When you're aroused during sex, the muscles in your groin/genital area start to flood with blood, making them engorged and tense (but in a good way). During orgasm, this tension is released (that's why a penis gradually becomes flaccid again afterwards, though it may take a little while), and at the same time a flood of hormones is released. The two things together create a rush of pleasurable sensation which is especially powerful in your genitals (you might feel involuntary muscle contractions) but can make you feel good all over too. Actually, you know what best sums up the feeling?

If you find yourself wondering whether you've had an orgasm, it's possible that you haven't yet, because you'll likely know it when you feel it, but remember that what orgasm looks and feels like in real life may be very different from what you've seen in films or porn. Just because you haven't seen stars, hit the ceiling, felt your head swivel 360 degrees and seen steam come pouring out of your ears doesn't mean you haven't come 'properly'! Experimenting on your own when you feel completely relaxed is one of the best ways to work out how it feels for you and what you enjoy. There is no one definition of what an orgasm feels like – it might feel quite different on different occasions.

One thing that doesn't vary, though, is the importance of contraception (birth control) and sexual health protection. There's so much info about this that I'm only going to give a whistle-stop tour, but you can get the full lowdown online on the NHS website, or by getting confidential advice from a sexual health clinic, or your GP.

In a nutshell, you should always use contraception unless you're actively planning to get pregnant, and you should always use STI protection unless you're actively planning to get an STI.

There are loads of contraceptive options (FIFTEEN in fact!) from the pill to the injection (ouch, but lasts for several months) to the implant (lasts three years), and they're mostly available freely and confidentially, even if you're under sixteen.

You can get pregnant from any genital-to-genital contact, if one person has a penis and the other has a vagina. You can get pregnant from a penis being inserted in the vagina, even if it's only for a few moments, even if it's 'just the tip', even if you pull out before ejaculating – because 'pre-cum' (a small amount of liquid that can appear at the tip of a penis when it's excited) contains sperm. But you can't get pregnant from oral sex (including swallowing semen) or manual sex (fingering/hand jobs), kissing, dry humping (through clothes) or mutual masturbation (when you're both touching yourselves at the same time. Way sexier than it sounds).

KEY FACT: Most contraceptives DO NOT protect you from STIs, so you need to use BOTH a contraceptive *and* a sexual health protection option each time you have sex. The only all-star multi-taskers that protect you from both pregnancy and STIs are condoms, but these can occasionally split, or come off, so it's well worth using one of those other fifteen contraceptive methods AS WELL AS a condom for extra, added precautions. (Well, you wouldn't go skydiving without a backup parachute, would you?)

It is safe to have sex on your period, but there is still a risk of STIs and a small risk of pregnancy so all the usual precautions apply. Guys who are 'grossed out' about having sex with women on their periods need to girl up. They need to think twice about whether they enjoy having blow jobs or ejaculating during sex. If women can put up with their bodily fluids, why shouldn't they put up with ours? Double standards much?

You can get STIs from oral sex or genital-to-genital contact, including vaginal and anal intercourse, and there's a small risk from manual sex, which increases if one or both partners lick their hands or put them in their mouths after touching genitals. Exposure to sores, open wounds or blood (including menstrual blood) increases the risk of STIs. If you are worried you might have an STI (much like if you suspect you might have mice, or enjoy the music of Justin Bieber) it's always safest to get it checked out asap before the problem gets worse.

Symptoms could include pain when you pee; itching, burning or tingling genitals; blisters, sores, lumps or spots on the genitals; green, yellow or smelly discharge; bleeding between periods and pain during sex. Or a past partner ringing you up and telling you they have an STI. But remember, some STIs have no obvious symptoms so if you've had unprotected sex, you'll still need to get checked.

You can get tested at:

- Your GP
- A sexual health clinic or genitourinary medicine (GUM) clinic
- Some community contraceptive clinics
- Some young people's sexual health services (call the Sexual Health Line on 0300 123 7123)

If a condom does come off or split, you have sex without protection (or an angel comes and has a chat with you) and you find yourself pregnant, try not to panic. You still have loads of options, and a GP, someone at your local sexual health clinic or a counsellor on a confidential advice line can talk them through with you (details in the back of the book). If it isn't the right time for you to have a child, the morning-after pill can be taken up to three days (seventy-two hours) after unprotected sex and you can get it free from all the places listed above, plus:

- Brook centres
- Some pharmacies
- Most NHS walk-in centres (England only)
- Some hospital accident and emergency (A&E) departments

It's great that types of emergency contraception are available, but don't rely on these chaps as regular contraception, OK? That would be like Man Utd never putting out their first team players and just relying on their reserves, which is silly because they're not nearly as talented and you'll probably get beaten by Wigan Athletic. Is that what you want? Well, is it? I didn't think so. You also have options later on in pregnancy, which can be discussed at your GP or through an organisation like the British Pregnancy Advisory Service, who can provide support and counselling as well as helping you to arrange an abortion if that's what you choose. You and only you have the right to decide what happens to your body and whether you want to go through with a pregnancy.

(If you're reading this in Ireland, the law is different, and abortion is illegal. But it's not against the law to seek advice about unplanned pregnancy, from an organization like Reproductive

Choices in Dublin, and it's also not illegal to travel abroad, say to the UK, for example, for an abortion.)

If you're sexually active you should go for regular sexual health checks. In fact, this is something you should always do before having sex with a new partner, just to be completely safe. Think of it like a car's MOT – if you can't guarantee the safety of your vehicle, you have no right being out on the road. But don't display the results of your STD test in a plastic disc on your chest because that would be weird and embarrassing for everybody.

It might feel awkward to have the conversation about getting sexual health checks with a new partner before you've slept together, but I promise you it is a *lot* less awkward than the 'what are these itchy purple mushrooms growing out of my vagina?' conversation. By a long way.

While I was writing this book and spending a lot of time alone at home (this isn't going where you think it is, although it does involve a pussy), a cute little ginger cat started showing up at my back door (oh, stop it) and mewing to be let in. She was a bit bigger than a kitten, with gorgeous green eyes and a white tip to her tail and I fell for her hook, line and sinker. So I sent a picture of her to my friends, one of whom replied, 'Watch out in case she has fleas.' And I was all like, 'Oh no, she's so cute and fluffy, she doesn't look like she has fleas,' 70 per cent because it was true and 30 per cent because I didn't know what to do if a cat has fleas and I thought that if I didn't think about it it would go away (which, for the record, is literally the exact opposite of what to do if a cat has fleas).

So she started hanging out with me while I was writing and I named her Moth (because she was quiet and flitty and she came around at night) and she would rub her face against the corner of my laptop screen and purr and rub her body against the legs of my chair. (Yes, smartarse, I can now see with the benefit of hindsight how the constant scratching up against things may have been a clue, OK?)

By the time I started feeling itchy it was too late. And even though I could show Moth the door, the infestation was already established. If you're wondering why I'm telling you all this, the moral of the story is: if you're thinking about getting snuggly with someone, make sure they get tested, even if they say it's fine, or claim they don't need to; even if they're adorable and they don't look like the type to be infected; even if their cute little face looks like this:

DO NOT FALL FOR IT! Excuse me real quick while I go apply some more anti-itching cream.

Like with sexual health, it's also every sexual participant's responsibility to take care of contraception – it shouldn't just be one partner's job or the other. Don't let your partner wriggle off the hook. This is something you should be discussing together. It's quite common for girls to report male partners complaining about having to wear a condom, saying it lessens the sensation, or makes them feel less intimate. This is a common CONunDrOM. (No? OK.) Sometimes a guy might argue he doesn't need to use a condom because he'll just 'pull out' before he ejaculates, or because you're on your period. These are terrible excuses and he shouldn't get away with them.

1. There are brilliant condoms available including feather-light varieties that can feel just as natural as not using one at all.
2. He can't be sure he'll pull out in time, and even if he does, there are still sperm present in 'pre-cum', which is the small amount of liquid that comes out of the penis before ejaculation.
3. Is it really worth the risk? Seriously, is it?
4. Even if there was no risk of pregnancy, you still need a condom to protect from STIs.
5. If all else fails, just remind him that having sex with a condom on feels a hell of a lot nicer than not having sex at all, which is his only other option.

If you can bear it, the NHS has a video on their website to help with this conversation, though they unfortunately chose to call it 'condom negotiation' which sounds way too similar to hostage negotiation. 'Just put the condom on and nobody has to get hurt. Put it on and I'll have a helicopter and half a million in unmarked bills ready outside. Just put it on *goddammit.*'

Also, if you need to know how to use one there are tons of great tutorial videos online, but just remember, it's like getting the last bit of toothpaste out of the tube: pinch the top and roll it down. Say it with me now: pinch the top and rooollll it down. (Pinch the top of the condom, that is, not the top of his willy. That would just be mean.)

Don't use a really old condom, even if he's carried it in his wallet since he was twelve; it's not romantic, it's gross. Don't use one that's already been used, or left in the sun. And don't tear it open with your teeth. Come on now.

For oral sex involving a vagina or anus, you can use a dental dam, which is a square piece of latex, kinda like a condom but flat. In fact, you can make your own by simply cutting a condom open. Dental dams get a bad rep for not being sexy, probably because they're the least sexily named thing ever, but using one is really not that big of a deal, and it protects from STIs when giving oral sex. So really you have to ask yourself what is more inconvenient – a moment of putting a square of latex in place, or herpes?

Lube or lubricant is a jelly-like substance sold in sex shops, pharmacies, some supermarkets and online. Lube is every sexual participant's best friend. Some people worry that using it means their vagina isn't producing enough natural lubrication, or that they're not turned on enough, but this isn't true at all – amounts of lubrication produced by the vagina vary massively and adding extra only makes things feel even better. Think of sex like one of those massive inflatable water slides at the funfair or the waterpark: too much friction can cause irritation and chafing, which tends to put a real downer on the moment, whereas the more slippery and slidey things are, the better the experience. Lube is also great for manual sex of any kind and is essential for anal sex, because the anus is delicate and doesn't self-lubricate, so can easily get sore or even tear without plenty of extra lube. It's important to use a lube that is water-based not oil-based as oil-based lube (and other things like Vaseline or baby oil) can damage condoms.

In fact, since it's come up, a note about anal sex:

Because it appears in so much heterosexual porn, it can feel like there's a lot of pressure for girls to do it and for guys to want to do it.

a) Not everyone does. According to the National Survey of Sexual Attitudes and Lifestyles, taken in 2000, 12.3 per

cent of men and 11.3 per cent of women had had anal sex in the past year.
b) You shouldn't ever be pushed into it, it's your choice.
c) Anyone of any gender who wants to can do it, it doesn't change your sexuality.
d) Some people really enjoy it, but others may find it painful, or just not their cup of tea.

Anybody who says you have to do it because they really want you to, or it will 'prove' how much you love them, or everyone else is doing it, or it's better for them because it'll feel tighter, is (ironically) talking out of their ... Nobody who makes you feel pressured deserves to have any kind of sex with you. You do not 'owe' anything to anyone.

If somebody is having vaginal penetrative sex with you and then suddenly withdraws and tries to penetrate you anally without warning or without your consent, this is a form of sexual assault. There is *no* rule that once you start having sex someone can do whatever they want without your agreement. (Remember the ice cream. Asking for a scoop of raspberry ripple does not mean you're also agreeing to eat one of mint choc chip.) In fact, you can say stop at any time and a partner legally HAS to respect that and stop, otherwise it's rape. Trying it once doesn't give your partner the right to keep doing it afterwards if you decide you don't want to.

Hopefully, this clears up a lot of questions, but for anything else I haven't covered, you should never feel too embarrassed to ask your GP absolutely anything, and there's brilliant advice and information available online, on sites like Scarleteen, Sexetc and Brook.

Finally, with any kind of sex, there might be an embarrassing moment or two. That's completely, utterly normal. If you don't have the odd embarrassing moment, you're probably not having sex. You might think the odd squelch or smell or mishap sounds embarrassing and terrifying, but flip the script for a second: how incredibly close do you end up feeling to someone who you've experienced those very, very intimate moments with? If anything, I think those things bring you even *closer*.

In sexually embarrassing situations, there are several things that it is comforting to remember. The first is that the person you are with really likes you a very great deal. They wouldn't be here if they didn't. So whatever it is that's come up (or *hasn't* come up), chances are you can deal with it together and maybe even laugh over it. Second, if you feel embarrassed, think about how you'd react if it was the other way around – you'd just want to put your partner at ease and reassure them. The chances are they feel the same way about you. Third, and perhaps most comforting of all, remember someone else has almost DEFINTELY been in a more embarrassing sex situation than you.

I have friends (who shall remain nameless) who have IRL experienced the following during sex:

- An extraordinarily loud fart
- An earlier than expected period
- Mid-coital discovery by parents
- A chipped tooth
- Semen in the eye
- Being pooped on by a seagull (don't even ask)

Luckily, sex isn't about making the perfect movie montage, it's about enjoying yourself with someone you completely trust. In none of the above cases did it mark the end of their relationship. (And, in most cases, it didn't even mark the end of the sex session either!)

So when the time is right, on your terms, just relax, enjoy yourself, and watch out for seagulls.

CHAPTER TEN

CIRCLE OF SHAME

It was whilst attending audition after audition that I first started to smell a sexist rat about the way women are portrayed on screen. When you're a struggling actor, your agent will send you to dozens of advert auditions, for the simple reason that if you are cast in an advert, you make a silly amount of money for only a few days' work. So I sat through more of these things than I can count, and in the process started to realize that there was something not-so-subtle going on in the way the industry both portrayed and treated men and women.

I turned up at a casting call for a wardrobe advert and sat nervously in the room, practising my lines under my breath for fifteen minutes before someone clapped me on the shoulder and jovially informed me as I went through the audition room door: 'We've decided to sex it up a bit and now you're taking your top off.'

My boyfriend, who was also an actor, would get long casting calls before he went to auditions, telling him exactly what they were looking for in the part, what the character was like and who they felt would be best suited to play him. They often looked something like this:

An architect; sensitive and doesn't form relationships easily, perhaps due to a traumatic past (his parents both died in a car accident when he was ten years old). Very much a loner who finds it hard to relate to others. Has to have a sense of vulnerability, and finds it difficult to trust, although once he does become close to somebody, he is fiercely loyal and will defend them to the death. Has a particular love of dogs and all animals – trusts them perhaps even more than humans.

I would also get casting breakdowns. They often looked something like this:

32DD.

I'm not even kidding. Here are some real-life casting breakdowns I received:

Mid-twenties, fresh, innocent (Keira Knightley-ish), lots of cleavage.

✳

The Damsel should be wearing a long, flowing dress that accentuates her cleavage. She needs to look sexy and attractive. [Are you starting to see the common theme?]

✳

Sara should have a playing age of early twenties to early thirties. Sara is a bright, intelligent, attractive woman who should have a wholesome 'girl next door' appeal rather than be an outright femme fatale. She is sexy and attractive, but in an understated, rather than in your face way. She should appeal to both men and women.

※

Pretty but not threatening.

※

Julia is a sixteen-year-old girl of stunning beauty. She's versatile. On the one hand, she's charismatic, sensual, in advance for her age. On the other hand, she's perfectly well-behaved and docile.

※

A beautiful, alluring, Lolita kind of woman. A sweet, innocent, stunner of a young woman who will eat your heart out if you come too close.

※

And my personal favourite . . .

Sexy Nun: 18–25, very good curvaceous physique.

Unfortunately, these examples are a pretty accurate indicator of what the media seems to think of women, and especially young women. Some recent research into the portrayal of women in film showed that only around 28 per cent of speaking roles in major Hollywood films are female, and a third of women in films are sexualized. Women in films are three times more likely than men to be shown partially naked. And for younger women, the picture is even starker – a huge 57 per cent of teenage girls in Hollywood films in 2012 were sexualized.[1]

Holy misogyny, Batman!

A big part of the problem is that the big, blockbuster films that everyone sees are almost completely written and directed by men. Of the top grossing 250 US films of 2014, just 17 (or 6.8 per cent) were directed by women, and only 11 per cent of the writers were female.[2]

And either these mostly male writers and directors have only ever met four women in their whole lives (one gorgeous, flawless teenage virgin, one very wise nun, one damaged and vengeful rape victim and one massive-breasted 'slut'), or they've wised up to the fact that there's money to be made from presenting women in the media as stereotypes.

There's a very simple and famous test to check just how sexist a film is. It's called the Bechdel test, and it was conceived by the American cartoonist Alison Bechdel. To pass the test, a film simply has to have at least two female characters, who talk to each other about something other than a man. Sounds like a pretty low bar, right? Well, according to the Bechdel website, a stunning 44 per cent of the films in its database at the time of writing (including hits like *Fantastic Four*, *22 Jump Street* and *Amazing Spider-Man 2*) fail to pass the test. A test so ludicrously simple that it literally would only require Brittney to turn to Tiffany and say, 'OMG, I just LOVE your cherry shortcake,' to pass with flying colours.

Even when we do get to hear from female characters, the more you think about it, the more you start to realize that the films and TV you're seeing are presenting you with the same caricatures over and over again, in very slightly different guises. Like the English Rose. Or the thin, slightly nagging, wholesome but sexy mom from *Modern Family, The OC, Gossip Girl, 90210* and pretty much every teen drama series ever. Or the sexy but sweet Asian sidekick. Or the 'sassy', exotic black girl who's usually just a brief obstacle between the hero and the white virgin types who he eventually falls in love with. (Yep, the stereotypes can be racial too.) The fat, pearl-clutching matron. The beautiful, sexy victim who needs rescuing to provide character development for the male hero. The crazy old cat lady. The popular, bitchy mean-girl cheerleader. The unpopular girl who whips off her glasses and takes her hair down and suddenly floors everybody with how shockingly, unexpectedly sexy she is. Because nobody saw that coming. The career ball-breaker who's too busy for love until it (literally) crashes into her and melts her secretly-girly-on-the-inside heart.

In a way, you can see why film and TV show makers feel the need to stick to the same stereotypes that we all know ~~and love~~. It makes it much easier to name the films. Imagine if they started being honest about women and relationships – they'd have to start using much longer titles, and they just wouldn't be as catchy.

Jurassic Sausage Fest

Indiana Jones and the totally unrealistic relationship with a woman who never would have slept with him in a million years after he was so mean to her

Ten Things I Hate About your unrealistic media-mandated beauty standards

Star Trek Into gratuitous nudity

Anna – how can this movie not pass the Bechdel test when it's literally all about a woman? – Karenina

The Hobbit: An Unexpected lack of female characters

Pretty – intelligent, self-sufficient – Woman

Game of oh good, another rape scene that's not even in the original book

500 Days of how unfair it is that a girl isn't into you

Armagedding real tired of being left at home with tears in my eyes while the men go off and do shit

It's not just on screen that we see this phenomenon of men creating a distorted picture of the world – we see it in the print media too, where women only write one in five front pages, and in the music industry, which is also heavily controlled by men.

Have you ever noticed any difference between the music videos of female singers and male singers?

Anything?

TRICK QUESTION – they all look pretty much the same: the girls are nearly naked and writhing around being sexy while the men are in suits and in control, regardless of whose video it is ... seem fair?

We also see it in adverts (which trick us even further by pretending that the people in them are totally real and natural like you and me and just happen to eat their cereal whilst grinning like a maniacal squirrel and dancing on the kitchen table).

In fact, with adverts, it goes so far that you have to start to wonder if they've all just run out of ideas.

Advertising Guy 1: So the first product to discuss today is a lawn mower. Any thoughts?

Advertising Guy 2: Uh, that's a tricky one. We could do something about how sharp it is?

Advertising Guy 3: Or maybe how it cuts really well?

The Only Advertising Lady in the Company: *(tentatively)* *opens mouth*

Advertising Guy 2: Milk, no sugars – thanks

The Only Advertising Lady in the Company: No, actually, I'm an advertiser too. I was just going to say, what about a clever twist on the Hungry Hippo game, where we see four lawn mowers all facing off against each other from opposite sides of a lawn, revving their engines and then they hungrily start munching up the grass, showing the speed and efficiency of the machine but also giving a sense of glamour and an edge to the product?

Silence

Advertising Guy 1: Hang on, chaps, hang on, I'm having an idea . . . What if there's a *woman* pushing the mower . . . In a BIKINI.

High-fives and backslapping all round

Advertising Guy 3: FANTASTIC, Fred, just fantastic. How does he do it?

Advertising Guy 2: Back of the net.

Advertising Guy 1: OK, item two, a new breakfast cereal.

Advertising Guy 2: Oh man, that's a real headscratcher.

The Only Advertising Lady in the Company: We could go with a bright cartoon design?

Advertising Guy 3: *(Talking over her)* Something about crunchiness?

Advertising Guy 1: Or, like, flavour?

Advertising Guy 2: Hey guys! What if we go with a bright cartoon design?

Advertising Guy 1: WOW man! Totally awesome idea.

Advertising Guy 3: I mean that is genius. Sheer genius.

The Only Advertising Lady in the Company: *Throws shade*

Advertising Guy 1: Or, actually, just a second ... I'm having a
   light bulb moment ... what if we ... what if we just do an ad
   where each of the pieces of cereal is a little floating boob, just
   bobbing around in the milk there?

High-fives and whoops all round

Advertising Guy 2: Yes! That's a much better idea!

Advertising Guy 3: Brilliant. Totally brilliant.

The Only Advertising Lady in the Company: But ...

Advertising Guy 1: Now, this final product is a bit trickier ... it's
   a new data storage software solution for multi-channel blue
   chip transcontinental corporations.

Pause

Advertising Guy 2: *(slowly)* Hang on a minute, we could ... it's
   coming to me ... Maybe we could ... no ... yes, wait, yes!
   Shall we put a pair of tits on a billboard?

The room erupts in ecstatic applause

The Only Advertising Lady in the Company: &#£%$#&

Honestly, it really makes you wonder about the recruitment process for jobs in advertising:

Interviewer: So ... how do you feel about breasts ... ?

It probably sounds like I'm exaggerating, right? People wouldn't keep just using tits like that willy-nilly to sell totally unrelated products ... there has to be *some* relevance. And wouldn't it eventually get kind of old?

OK, see if you can guess what these adverts have been used

to sell (it shouldn't be too hard, right? Given that adverts are supposed to, ya know, *advertise* the product and all):

1. A headless woman's body with two pairs of breasts, one on her front and one on her back
2. A picture of a woman's top with one erect nipple
3. A photo of four women all pressing their breasts together. Oh, and you can't see their faces, because why would you need to?
4. A man standing with his foot pressing down on a woman's neck
5. A woman in a corset and stockings holding a gun
6. A topless woman with a towel not quite covering her butt crack
7. A naked woman covering her breasts with a placard
8. A sexy woman in a French maid costume
9. A woman in a very low-cut, cleavage-enhancing bra
10. A topless woman in a thong

'Underwear?' I hear you cry. 'Perhaps some kind of full-body moisturising cream?'

Well, no.

Answers:

1. A games console
2. A car
3. A car
4. A dress
5. Office space for rent
6. Drinking water
7. Bus fares

8. Foreign currency exchange

9. Mascara

10. An internet server

Did you get them all right?

Once you start to see it, the ridiculousness is breathtaking. And so are the double standards . . .

Just look at the way headlines about men getting new business jobs are written:

Sir Mike Rake Becomes RAC Chairman

Funding Circle Appoints Wall Street Heavyweight Robert K. Steel

Allan Leighton to be Chairman at Peacocks

. . . compared to this headline from the very same national newspaper about a woman in an identical position:

Mother of Three Poised to Lead the BBC

Hmmm, one of these things is not like the others.

Just look at the way new male cabinet ministers are discussed in the press, compared to new female ministers:

Sajid Javid Appointed Business Secretary

Philip Hammond Stays on as Foreign Secretary

＊

Thigh-flashing Esther and the Battle of the Downing St Catwalk

Now Win Election, PM Tells New Girls

Just look at the way we treat the leaders of our political parties according to their gender; like Nicola Sturgeon facing cartoons of her cleavage, and her face Photoshopped onto an image of a scantily clad woman on a wrecking-ball, let alone headlines about her 'baby hopes' and her 'style transformation'.

It's clever, because we think of the media as reflecting the world around us, so it's very powerful in convincing us that this is 'the way things are' and the way we are expected to behave and look, when in reality the media reflects the childish and narrow fantasies of a very small group of very powerful men.

When someone creates a convincing illusion of what the world is like, the only way to see that it's fake is to go up and poke the edges. We know this from the bit where Jim Carrey sails his boat right into the fake sky in *The Truman Show,* and also from how in the second *Hunger Games,* Katniss can see the fuzzy bits at the edges of the force field in the arena. It's the same with the media: you can only tell it's not real when you look at the scrappy, peeling edges; the bits that are a bit dirty and rubbish and desperately need refurbishing but nobody can really be bothered.

This is the giveaway – the big reveal – the slipping of the mask – the hole where the cat gets out of the bag. This is where we realize that what's being packaged and presented to us as 'reality' is actually not news at all. We can see it in the headlines that are barely scraped together into 'stories' as an excuse to show thirty close-up unflattering or sexy photographs:

Rosanna Arquette Makes a Face After Taking a Sip
of a Healthy Juice Drink

Lauren Goodger Narrowly Avoids Walking into a Puddle
During Day Out in Essex

Kopycat Khloe Strikes Again! Youngest Kardashian Shows
Off Her Tummy in a Tight Green Keyhole Dress ... Almost a
Year After Her Sister Kim Wears Near Identical Frock

Hilary Duff Glows After Gym Visit Despite Wearing
Drab T-shirt and Funky Leggings

Posh Behind Bars ... But Don't Worry It's Just
Victoria Beckham Behind Some Railings

We see it in the stereotypes and the clichés and the exaggeration:

Are All Beautiful Women Boring?

Older Women: Should They Be Classy or Brassy?

Women Really Listen Only to Gossip and Other People's
Conversation, Study Reveals

Why Women Become Less Bitchy as They Get Older
(And Yes, It's to Do with Men)

Girls Whose 'Career' Choice Is Pregnancy

We see it in the outright contradictions:

Stop Portraying Teens as Sexual Objects

Teenager Elle Fanning Shows Off Her Womanly Curves

*

Music, Videos and Clothing Are Sexualizing Our
Children, Warns Rape Centre Boss

Hard to Believe She's Just 16! Kendall Jenner
Looks Older Than Her Years as She Shows Off Her
Model Shape in Stunning Bikini Shoot

✻

Crackdown Urged on Sexual Imagery

Strike a Pose! Chloe Sims Is full of Confidence as She Shows Off
Her Ample Assets in Steamy New Lingerie Shoot

✻

Too Old for a Two-Piece? 39 Is the Age at Which
Women Should Give Up Bikinis For Good

Women Over 40 Should Wear Bikinis, Says Nancy Dell'olio,
Aged 50 (And She Should Know)

✻

Women Should Stop Chasing Elusive Images

How to Look Like a Wag: Coleen's Trainer Reveals
Secrets to a Slimmer Figure

✻

Should 40-Something Women Like Madonna
Start Dressing Their Age?

Madonna Looks Incredibly Youthful in Sexy Ad for Skincare Line

✻

And most of all we see it in the way that girls, under the age of
eighteen, are creepily and lecherously served up as nothing but
sex objects:

Growing Up Fast! Ariel Winter, 15, Dresses Older Than
Her Age In A Low-Cut Top And Towering Heels

Glamour Girl! Chloe Moretz, 16, Is All Grown Up

Elle Fanning Looks All Grown Up at 13

I would go on, but if you put 'all grown up' into the search bar on one national tabloid website alone it comes up with 26,991 results, and I've got a few other things to say in this book.

It's not surprising that other folk who don't look exactly like the media moguls get a bad rep too – immigrants, people of colour, people with disabilities, sex workers, people on benefits, LGBT* folk and so on. Think about how the media paints these groups and you start to realize that you're just seeing the same one person over and over again – the same stereotype of the fierce, exotic, sexy black woman or the heart-warming disabled 'striver' . . . the same wise-cracking Asian sidekick or scrounging benefit fraudster. You start to realize that lesbians on screen are either stereotypically butch or hyper-sexualized for the straight male gaze; that large women are the butt of jokes and trans characters only appear in storylines *about* being trans, never because that just happens to be their character's identity.

And the more false, unrealistic stereotypes about women and girls are perpetuated and repeated in the media all around us, the more they contribute to an unshakeable idea that they represent the realities of women and girls and the way we 'ought' to be.

Once we know what the 'perfect' woman looks like, we have to learn how to play the part . . . Step forward, women's magazines.

As a girl, the world (by which I mean the media) will send you a shit ton of very convincing messages about what you should and should not wear, eat, do, like, read, watch, say, and rub into your neck.

One of the problems with magazines is that they have to come up with something new to write each month, and they deal with a fairly narrow range of topics, which means that they inevitably end up repeating and contradicting themselves, so it is very difficult to follow their advice, even if you wanted to. You just end up getting *really* confused ...

- If you're doing a no-fruit diet to avoid the sugars in fruit where does that leave you on the whole 'drink hot water with lemon every morning or the world will end' mantra?

- If camel toe is a fashion disaster but skinny jeans are in is it better to risk the former or unfashionably avoid the latter?

- If the cover of a magazine says 'Curves Are Back!' one week but 'Amazing Celeb Bikini Weight Loss' the next, which part of myself am I supposed to hate?

- If one issue of a magazine has a quiz called 'Is He Going to Cheat?' and the next has an article called 'How Not to Be a Crazy Jealous Girlfriend', who's the crazy one now?

- If one magazine says the Atkins diet is in and the other asks if red meat is the Devil, can I just eat all the bacon and pretend I didn't understand the question?

So many questions, so little time.
I mean, literally, come on, people. COME ON!
The trouble with all this is that it adds up. Media is everywhere. The newspaper that flaps open on the seat next to you on the tube. The advert that pops up on your mobile phone screen. The TV, the films, the magazines: together they create a world that swallows you whole, and once you tumble in it's almost impossible to get out again. It affects everything.

MEDIA
gorgeous curves
Sexy
STYLE MAG
CLEAVAGE
perfect
THIGH GAP
PERFECTION!
SLIM · TONED · HIP
HOT + thin
Beauty
BUSTY · TANNED
glossy silky soft

You fall into a world that has its own codes and labels, values and symbols, even its own language.

A GLOSSARY OF TERMS FOR WOMEN'S MAGAZINES AND TABLOIDS

Flaunts – has body part
Shows off – has body part
Curvaceous – has body part
Outshines – stands next to
Dresses down – isn't attending film premiere
Steals the show – stands next to
Puts on a display – leaves the house
Highlights – has
Showcases – has
Goes bare-faced – is human
Goes make-up free – is human
Busty – has breasts
Cosies up to – stands near
Opens up – is asked invasive questions about
Slips into – wears
Pours curves into – wears
Covers up – wears coat
Displays – has body part
Leggy – has legs
Steps out – leaves house

Of course, as soon as you complain about any of this, you instantly hear cries of: 'well, women are asking for it', 'well, she was flaunting it' and 'well, what did she expect dressed like that?'

You know the phrase 'don't shoot the messenger'? That can be directly adapted to 'don't shoot the model'. Or the stripper. Or the pole dancer. Or Miley Cyrus. (I mean this both metaphorically and literally, because you should never shoot anyone, OK?)

The pole dancer didn't invent the pole. The model didn't come up with the idea of only making designer samples in a size that only 0.0001 per cent of women can wear. Miley Cyrus didn't build the wrecking ball (though if she did, that is impressive because she is one tiny, little person).

These women are the symptoms, not the causes, of a world which sends women the message that their only worth and value lies in their bodies, looks and sexiness.

Remember, research shows five years old is the age when girls first start to worry about their size and feel they are too fat. FIVE. YEARS. OLD.

We don't hear things when we are five and stop to carefully and analytically weigh up their accuracy. We accept them and they become part of the framework we are building in our head called 'the world'. I don't mean this patronisingly. I'm not saying women are stupid or being duped, though I think we are all being duped, at least a little bit. What I am saying is that we can't take the framework out of the picture. If taking off our clothes, or making our bodies a lot smaller than they naturally would be, or dancing around a pole were things that people independently, spontaneously came up with and thought were fun, empowering ideas, then we'd be seeing equal numbers of men and women doing them. And we're not. So there must be something else going on.

We can't drop girls and women into this world that sidelines and stereotypes and criticizes and shames them, and then point hysterically at them and cry foul when they go along with some of the expectations we force upon them. It's also a clever way for the real culprits – the structural sexism, and the institutions that support it – to escape quietly out the back door while we blame the wrong people. It's misdirection. It's sleight of hand. Don't let it fool you.

Of course, the media isn't all bad.

One great thing about teen magazines is that they have really helpful quizzes that can aid you in making important life decisions, discovering vital new skills and finding out some deep shit about yourself that you never knew before.

Here are some real life examples:

- Which of Taylor Swift's Exes is Right for You?
- What's Your Dating Superpower?
- Are You Too Needy?
- Is He Going to Dump You?
- Which Haircut Matches Your Personality?
- Why Don't You Have a Boyfriend and Why Are You Single? (presumably same answer)
- Who is Your Celebrity Best Friend?
- What is Your Perfume Personality?

Now I know what you're thinking. Knowing your perfume personality could actually change your life in a number of meaningful ways. Unfortunately I never got as far as finding out what mine was (flirty, sexy, chic or sweet), because I got distracted by a link to 'Seven Game-Changing Mascara Techniques You've Probably Never Considered Before'. And you know what? I had *not* considered them before.

The trouble with magazine quizzes is that they suggest things can be sorted into easy, clear boxes, when life, and feelings, and personality, and relationships and, well, pretty much everything, doesn't really work that way.

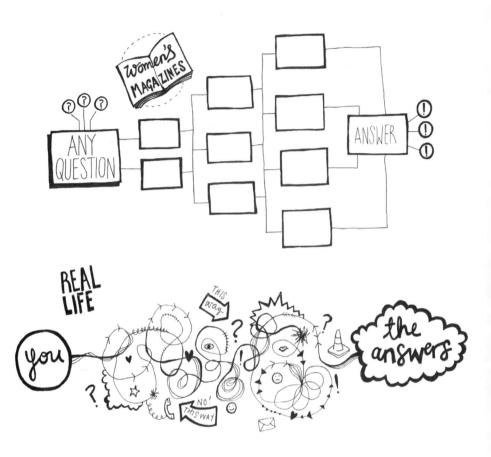

Alongside the notion that there is a simple solution to every problem because we are all the same (and just need to buy more face cream) go articles with titles like 'Ten Things Every Girl Should Know How to Do'. These make me want to burn everything. So here are some genuine examples from original versions of such articles, alongside an alternative list:

Ten Things Every Girl Should Know How to Do According to Magazines	Ten Things Every Girl Should Know How to Do in Real Life
Drink apple cider vinegar (Why is this even on the list? Since when is drinking something a skill you need to learn how to do?)	Put apple cider vinegar in the bin
How to take a compliment	How to tell a guy to get lost if he's harassing you
How to walk in high heels	How to buy flip-flops
How to find the right haircut for your face shape	How to consider literally everything else in life before worrying about your 'face shape'
How to please your man in bed	How to instruct your partner exactly how to pleasure you in bed
How to kiss in a way that communicates perfectly what you would and wouldn't like to happen next	How to use your words and have an actual conversation, in the event that your partner doesn't, in fact, turn out to be lip-psychic
How to get bikini body ready	How to put a bikini on your body
How to lose half a stone in two weeks	How to feel great about your body in spite of the media

In fact, just to be sure, here's another list:

TOP TEN PIECES OF ADVICE YOU MUST IGNORE

1. Lie back and think of England

a) There is literally *no* situation in which this is good advice. You should never be pushed into thinking about England if you don't want to. (Or having sex.)

b) Who says you have to lie back during sex? Haven't they heard of doggy style/standing sex/spooning/girl on top/reverse cowgirl?

2. Dress for your figure

Are you actually an apple, a pear or an hourglass in real life? If yes, then I can see the merit in dressing to cover that up. If no, dress for yourself, goddammit! Your figure can deal with it. Life is way too short and clothes you like are way too hard to find for 'rules' about who can wear what.

3. Always please your man

a) You might not be attracted to men.

b) If you are, let's start with finding one who pleases *you*.

4. No carbs before Marbs

a) Being fit and healthy has nothing to do with cutting out carbs.

b) Enjoying your holiday has nothing to do with what you've eaten two weeks before.

c) Bikinis don't just come in one size.

d) Pizza always wins.

5. Keep your friends close and your enemies closer

This is a terrible piece of advice. Think about it. Why? Just why?

6. Don't get a reputation

Get a reputation. For being awesome.

7. Don't frown – you never know who might be falling in love with your smile

If they're worth falling for, they'll like you no matter what mood you're in. Also, fake smiles are the actual worst.

8. Learn to take a joke

If your joke was funny in the first place you wouldn't have to teach people to take it.

9. Don't intimidate a guy by being too smart

A guy who's worth his salt would find your intelligence
attractive, not off-putting. If this comes up, check whether
he's intimidated by other smart men.

10. Don't be the one to make the first move

OK, rule of thumb: if it doesn't apply with pizza, it's
probably wrong.

ALWAYS take the first slice of pizza. See? It totally works.

Other applicable situations:

A pizza pleases *you*. Not the other way around.

A pizza is rarely intimidated by your intelligence.

You should NEVER wait three days to call a pizza in case it
thinks you're desperate.

As easy as it is to make fun of magazines, and as often as they do
deserve it, this isn't really to say that all magazines are 'bad' or 'evil'
or that you shouldn't read them. You're not stupid, you can work out
for yourself what you want to read. You might really enjoy some of
the quizzes, or love the fashion, or the beauty tips. There are some
magazines that are making a real effort to think about issues like
body image and sexism and trying to deal with them through their
content and by using their platforms to profile more diverse women.

It's just that sometimes it's worth stopping to think about how
something's making you feel, especially if it's something you've
done for a long time without ever really taking stock. The reason
it's worth thinking about how magazines, particularly, make you
feel, is because research suggests they can have quite a negative
impact on young women's emotions. One study found that three
out of four teenage girls feel depressed, guilty and shameful after
spending just three minutes leafing through a fashion magazine.[3]

So next time you're flipping through a glossy, or reading, watching or listening to any form of media for that matter, try taking this simple test:

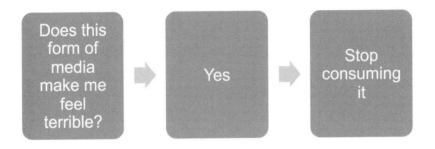

Does this form of media make me feel terrible? → Yes → Stop consuming it

This is actually extremely liberating. It's strange, when you think about it, that more of us haven't followed this stunningly simple logic already. But why haven't we? Because this stuff is EVERYWHERE! It's so normal that we just get used to how it makes us feel and plough on anyway.

Not to get all deep and meaningful on you, but we have so little time. We have to think carefully about what we choose to spend it on.

Something that ultimately makes you feel sad or worried or bad about yourself just doesn't deserve to come very high on the list. Especially when there are so many other options out there.

Looking for some great alternatives? Try *Rookie*, an awesome mag written for young women by young women, covering everything from fashion to female role models; *Ms* for feminism and current affairs; *Bitch,* which is funny, informative and on point; *Bust* for a fab mixture of craft, DIY and celeb interviews (not as weird as it sounds); or *Shameless,* which is packed with art, culture and current events and aimed at young women and trans youth. Also try: *Curve, Go, Lula, Diva* and *Frankie.*

We tend to think of the media as a mirror that reflects the world around us. But it's really a fairground mirror, which squeezes and stretches and distorts the picture, sometimes to the point where the truth is unrecognizable. So remember, the next time you see a headline, or an advert, or a picture, stop and consider the airbrushing, the bias and the hypocrisy. And above all, remember this: the answer to any question in a tabloid headline is almost always: NO.

CHAPTER ELEVEN

PORN ≠ SEX

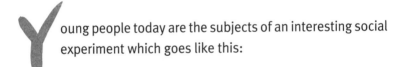

Young people today are the subjects of an interesting social experiment which goes like this:

1. Create millions of moving pictures of people having sex.
2. Make the pictures available to everyone, including children, at a single click.
3. Maintain a sense of dirty mystery about sex so these videos are watched in secret and nobody feels like they can talk about them or ask any questions.
4. React with astonishment when young people assume sex is identical to what they see in porn, and disapprove when they want to talk about it.

Luckily, the government has fixed this. They have worked out a cunning plan to fix it all:

They're turning off the porn.

Or more precisely, they've focused on trying to crack down on certain porn sites and put measures in place that *they think* will help prevent young people accessing porn. In the meantime though, just in case there are any unexpected glitches in that great plan...

People often treat sex as if it is something embarrassing, naughty or bad. People also often think that the best way to deal with something embarrassing, naughty or bad is to avoid talking about it, as if they can pretend it away altogether. This is probably the single most effective way to make any topic more interesting, exciting and alluring.

For example: WHATEVER YOU DO, DO NOT THINK ABOUT TAP-DANCING VAGINAS.

What are you imagining right now?

See?

When you combine not talking about sex very much in society with the idea that it is some huge, dangerous secret, you end up with people being a lot more likely to try and find out about sex on their own. Luckily, porn is on hand to provide an easy-peasy way of seeing what all the fuss is about.

Except there's a problem. What we see in porn isn't necessarily what a lot of real-life sex looks like, although it might be what some people happen to enjoy.

Think about how much people love to dance. It's a worldwide activity that billions of people enjoy and it's often something men and women do together in pairs, although there are also lots of other ways of doing it – on your own, in a group, with people of the same sex etc.

Now imagine dancing, whilst still hugely enjoyable and popular, is very taboo. It is not something you would do in public, even though it's accepted that most people do it a lot in private. It's a bit personal and embarrassing to talk about dancing openly. It makes people giggle and go red when it comes up. Imagine, basically, that dancing was treated the way we treat sex.

Now imagine that there are millions of videos online, easily accessible at the click of a mouse, that show people dancing.

Naturally, as a young person, you hear about dancing a lot and you feel excited about the idea that you'll do it one day. Maybe you experiment with it a little bit in your own bedroom. But you're not really sure what the moves are or how you should do them, since you've never seen anyone else do it. Everybody seems to be talking about it, but you're pretty sketchy on the details. So of course you go online to see these mysterious videos and find out what it's like.

Online, the choice is massive. There are literally millions of videos of people dancing. A lot of the people in the videos look very attractive and muscular and not that much like normal people, but you don't really stop to think about it. There are lots of different types of dancing around if you explore deeply enough, but you tend to click on the videos that come up most immediately, on the front pages and the biggest sites.

Almost every video you watch shows people dancing Gangnam Style.

There are quick, explosive Gangnam Style dances and long

Gangnam Style marathons, people who dance Gangnam Style alone and people who do it in threes, people who look like they're enjoying Gangnam Style and people who don't look like they're having a very good time at all. There are people who seem to be very strongly in control of their dance partner, people who make small talk first and people who go straight into it. Sometimes there's pizza. But overwhelmingly, the impression you get from watching the videos is that when you dance, you're expected to do Gangnam Style. That's the way it's done. That's what your dance partner will be expecting.

You get the impression that Gangnam Style is by far the most popular and normal dance in the world.

This is a bit like how it is with porn. We take one, very specific, narrow way of having sex and create a whole industry around it. We blast it out so many millions of times that if you look online you think that's what sex is, and how it's done, and how you'll be expected to do it.

But the thing is, as we know, most of the time not that many people dance Gangnam Style. Sure, some people enjoy it, and that's absolutely fine, but putting only Gangnam Style in most of the videos would give a really distorted and inaccurate idea of what dancing was like.

(PS If you don't know what Gangnam Style is, imagine a dance move that is about 40 per cent dance and 60 per cent trolling.)

(PPS Now you want to go and Google 'Gangnam Style', don't you? Go on, I'll wait.)

(PPPS Whatever you do, don't Google 'Gangnam Style porn'. Just don't. It could ruin sex for you forever.)

(PPPPS You're doing it right now, aren't you? Don't blame me, I tried to warn you.)

So, where were we?

Right. Seeing only videos of people doing Gangnam Style doesn't give you a very realistic idea of what dancing is.

That's what happens with porn.

So you learn that men are expected to have huge penises and women should be slim with huge breasts. You learn that the men are in control and the women are submissive.

You learn that women shouldn't have any body hair.

You learn that sex is often about humiliating or hurting women – smacking them or ejaculating in their faces or having several men dominating them at one time.

You learn that sex is something done by men to women.

There are about a gazillion porn sites on the internet, and they're not exactly difficult to find. Let's take a moment for a big round of applause. Human beings were given the internet, which provided them with almost infinite potential for invention and progress. They came up with millions and millions and millions of versions of putting a stick in a hole. (Of course that's not all that sex is, *obviously,* but you could be forgiven for thinking so if you looked at a lot of mainstream porn.)

So let's try it. Let's look at some porn.

Typing 'porn' into Google immediately brings up 381 million results, starting with the biggest and most popular porn websites like Porn Hub and Red Tube. (Hell, even if you mistype it, like I did at first and put in 'ponr', you *still* get over a million options.)

I click the top link.

On the front page of the site, before I've clicked anything else, I can see a running video, repeating on a loop. The first part of the video shows an unusually large (I'm talking salami) penis being quite forcefully jammed into a woman's anus. We can't see her face so it's unclear how she feels about this.

Then the video jumps to a picture of a woman on her hands and knees. We're seeing her from the front, so we can see her face, but not the face of the man kneeling behind her, entering her from behind. The main focus of the video is the woman's face, which is clearly screwed up in pain. She is holding a hand over her mouth as if she is trying not to cry out.

Before you can take it in, the video snaps to another woman, in the same position, this time screaming out in pain. The caption says: PunishTube.

So within a single click, without making any choices, the first porn content we've seen shows women screaming in pain and includes the word 'punish'. That's a pretty powerful suggestion of what sex is about.

The other video titles on the first page also give two fairly strong impressions: 1. This is about picking and choosing 'types' of women, and 2. It's about doing something quite 'hard' *to* them.

Titles include:

'Hot teen first assfuck'

'Tasting that granny punany'

'Teen gets fucked anal'

'Blonde teen cocksucker'

'Busty first timer fucked hard'

'Girl gets her asshole destroyed'

'Asian slut fucked hard'

'Blonde brutally gang fucked, choked'

None of the images on the videos shows the men involved – the close-ups are all on women's bodies and faces, and the video titles also focus on the women. One of the videos on the first page shows a man beating a woman hard around the face.

Words like 'slammed', 'nailed', and 'hard' come up again and again and many of the pictures show women's faces covered in semen. Some of the most common descriptions of the women include 'filthy whore', 'just over eighteen', 'slut', 'teen', 'milf'. The men are very rarely even mentioned.

That's because the men are the eyes behind the camera, the

assumed viewers. We're seeing porn which is overwhelmingly made by men, for men, from a male perspective. A lot of it is on a scale which starts at dominating a woman hard and ends with raping and hurting a woman. I couldn't find much in the area of kind, gentle, loving, mutual sex.

It's important to say, some people like rough sex. Some people engage in BDSM, which can include bondage and discipline, dominance and submission, sadism and masochism. This might involve one partner controlling another, ropes and restraints, and stuff like spanking among many other things. Some variants of these might look particularly rough from an outside perspective, but within the actual BDSM community, they're carried out within a strictly consensual framework, where an agreement has been made beforehand about exactly what people want to do, about the fact that these are their particular fantasies and that they can stop at any time using a 'safe' word.

The examples I'm talking about aren't BDSM videos. They're just mainstream videos that happen to focus on humiliating or punishing women.

If there were lots of other places to hear and learn about sex, the content on porn sites wouldn't matter. If the content on porn sites reflected the wide variety of actual sex people have, then the fact this is the only place we hear about sex wouldn't matter. But put the two together and we have one very specific group of people, who control the porn industry, telling the majority of young people what sex is. And that's a problem.

Personally, I disagree with the government. I think that if you look at these two factors, the one we are much more likely to be able to influence is not the existence of online porn, but the fact that we're not talking about sex anywhere else. Trying to stop people seeing porn is like trying to keep water in a sieve (not to mention the fact that it's controlling and dictatorial).

It's like there's a sieve with a million holes in it and they're trying to individually plug one hole at a time instead of just putting a bowl under it.

And the bowl is literally right there.

We have the bowl.

'The bowl' is dealing with the problems porn might create using helpful discussions about porn and sex – like in the classroom maybe – HEY, AWESOME PLAN!

What's that? You're going to carry on refusing to have compulsory sex and relationships education and just pretend that we can turn off all the porn? OK then.

As a result, I get emails from teenage girls saying that they're so scared to have sex they cry about it regularly, because they've seen a video on a boy's mobile phone at school and found out that 'when you have sex the woman has to be crying and hurting'. I've been to a school where I heard about a rape case involving a fourteen-year-old boy who, when asked by a teacher, 'Why didn't you stop when she was crying?', replied: 'Because it's normal for girls to cry during sex.'

I've started asking teenage girls at the schools I visit whether they think the boys in their year have seen porn. The answer is always: 'Yes. All of them.' The girls tend to think they watch a lot less porn than their male peers, but most of them have usually seen some, and they have a firm idea of the sort of thing they think the boys are watching. When I ask them whether they feel this has an impact on them, the same three words tend to crop up in their answers – 'assumptions', 'normal' and 'pressure'.

Assumptions that you'll be hairless and submissive. Normal to have pneumatic breasts. Pressure to do anal.

Because porn gives us ideas about what's 'normal'.

There's a definite feeling that porn is 'real'. Young people who write to me often describe porn as 'sex videos' or 'real-life sex'.

PORN

ラ
フ

SEXY

Weirdly, we don't do this with other types of films. We don't watch *Spider-Man* and go 'OMG, I *knew* there was something weird about that Andrew Garfield – he can shoot webs out of his wrists!' We don't watch *Star Wars* and think we can suddenly do Jedi mind tricks and fight lightsabre battles. We understand about stunt actors who are specially trained to do unusual things, and about lighting and make-up and clever camera angles. But with porn we somehow think it's real, and that we'll be expected to do it just like the people whose job it is to create the fantasy.

(Which is weird, when you consider how downright unrealistic many porn scenarios are. There's one whole site where every video involves a pizza delivery guy, and when the woman opens the box, the guy's penis is sticking up through a hole in the pizza . . . she is unfailingly *delighted* by this.)

A lot of the more easily accessible mainstream porn also tends to erase LGBT* folk by focusing on the 'man doing stuff to a woman' angle fairly obsessively – and even though you do see quite a lot of girl-on-girl porn, it tends to be more for a male viewer's enjoyment than a gay female audience. (Just look at the way they wiggle each other's clitorises around like they're trying to rub a smudge off a window pane . . .)

In fact, the more you look, the more differences you start to see between porn and real-life sex.

Porn	Real-life sex
People with nothing but sex on their mind who literally never have to do anything else.	Often has to fit in around annoying real-life things like essays, work, feeling bloated, not having a condom to hand, just not feeling it, seeing a massive spider on the ceiling earlier that day and being too scared to have sex because you don't know where it went and can't stand the idea of it abseiling down and landing on your back mid-coitus.
Always sexy, rarely funny, never embarrassing.	Not always sexy, often funny, sometimes embarrassing. (See: fanny farts, lost condoms, reluctant erections, trying to be supremely sexy in the shower and slipping over.)
Everyone seems to read each other's mind or else doesn't care whether they're into it or not. Reasons for having sex vary from 'This real estate agent is hot' to 'OMG, is that a penis in my pizza?'	Talking is sometimes required to work out what you each feel like doing and how.
Just looking at a woman turns her into a hot writhing pool of desire.	Somewhat more effort required, please.
Body parts are huge, shiny, firm and uniform.	Body parts are different sizes, sometimes jiggly or squishy, sometimes smaller but just as pleasurable! (Like Sainsbury's basics potatoes: different shapes and sizes, still just as tasty.)
Women just love to swallow.	Some women do, many don't, plus it carries a risk of sexually transmitted infections.
Multiple positions, multiple orgasms, multiple sessions.	Sometimes multiple things, sometimes once is enough and then we quite fancy a snuggle, a shower or a piece of peanut butter on toast, thanks very much.
Body hair entirely absent.	Body hair performs its initially intended function: Protecting. From. Friction.

Vulvas are identical, hairless and often without very visible labia.	Vulvas and labia come in an array of colours, sizes, shapes and lengths – don't take it from me, check out some of the lovely internet sites dedicated to them in all their joyful variety. (As one site put it, 'The ideal labia is your own', which is so true, because it wouldn't be very pleasurable at all to have sex using someone else's.)
Two women having sex are nearly always doing it to turn men on.	Two women having sex are nearly always doing it to turn *each other* on and definitely not for men's pleasure . . . that's kind of the whole point.
Foreplay optional as women love being entered suddenly with little warning or preparation and find it intensely erotic.	Foreplay extremely necessary to arousal and lubrication, entry before these are achieved can hurt like hell and is pretty much the exact opposite of sexy.
Sex can go on for hours at a time, remains incredibly sexy throughout.	Sex might end after only a few minutes, and can still be great. Times vary. See small print for details.
Simultaneous ejaculation is just the norm.	Simultaneous ejaculation is rare (please, this isn't an equation) and concentrating on pleasuring each other one at a time can be amazing.
Women climax from penetration only.	Most women require clitoral stimulation to climax.
Women squirt all over the place.	Some women do ejaculate but most don't. It's not a fountain and lights show, OK?
Maximum enjoyment comes from wildest, hardest sex, almost always ending up with anal sex, which the women totally dig.	All kinds of sex are enjoyable, including hard and fast, slow and sensual, and everything in between. Some people like anal sex, others don't.
Ejaculating on a woman's face can only earn you extra romance points because boy, do we love it.	Ejaculating on a woman's face might make it the last time you have sex in a verrrry long while unless she's explicitly asked you to.

However, the fact that mainstream porn doesn't reflect a great diversity of experiences doesn't mean that there's nothing else to go on. There is a fast-expanding list of websites offering 'ethical' porn, which claims to guarantee that the participants are being paid, well treated and are in no way coerced (an issue that's worth carefully thinking about with mainstream porn, where it is very difficult to be certain these things are the case). These sites, like 'make love not porn', for example, tend to have more varied body shapes, more realistic scenarios and angles, presenting sex between consensual partners who are interested in really pleasuring each other, and focusing more on mutual enjoyment than a performance for an audience. There's also a vast amount of erotica online that's specifically aimed at women, including the rather delightfully named 'Cliterature'. You can also find a lot of great erotic writing that's far more inclusive of a wide range of different sexualities, preferences and gender identities. Hurray!

But I know what you're thinking. Lots of girls are already aware porn isn't necessarily the same as real life sex. What about the boys? What if they're not reading this book? (Though, for the boys who are, HELLO! Happy to have you on board!)

You're right. We definitely need to talk to people of all genders about porn and sex and reality. While we could go out there and try and achieve this with some kind of roadshow, the chances are we'd miss a few people and we might get some funny looks. So, the simplest solution to guarantee we get the message out there to all young people would be (as previously mentioned) to put it on the curriculum. If you agree this is important, you can write to your MP and let them know.

In the meantime, we're going to have to girl up and talk about it. We need to have these conversations, and the people we most need to have them with are those we are likely to have sex with.

So how do you talk about porn with a partner?

There are lots of different ways to approach the subject and it doesn't have to be scary or feel like a monumentally unsexy public service message. The key thing is not to make it sound like you're making assumptions or criticizing, more that you just want to have an open discussion.

Some people find it easiest to bring in some context – if so, you might find some figures useful. For example, it's worth talking about porn and sex, because a BBC survey found that 60 per cent of people were aged fourteen or younger when they first saw porn online. The same study found that more than half the respondents thought that online pornography affects what young men and women expect from sex and 74 per cent thought it particularly affected men's sexual expectations.[1] So watching loads of porn might make it more difficult for you to enjoy real sex in the long run. Another good way to raise the topic without feeling negative or 'judgy' is to have a conversation about sexual fantasies and ideas you might like to try out. This could lead quite naturally into a discussion about what you or your partner might have seen online, and also gives you an opportunity to set boundaries and be clear about what you don't want to do, before you reach the heat of the moment.

Other people find it easier to break the ice in a funny way: 'We need to talk about porn and we can't have sex without talking about it, so speak now or forever hold your penis.'

However you approach it, the key things to chat about are how you both feel about porn, how it might impact on your relationship, and what sort of things you feel happen in porn that you might or might not want to replicate in your own sex life.

Above all, whether you choose to watch porn or not, whether your partner(s) watch it or not, just remember it doesn't necessarily reflect reality, and it doesn't have to influence your sex life unless you want it to, any more than *Big Brother* influences the way you treat your housemates or *Top Gear* influences the way you drive. Which hopefully is not at all. Unless you are Jeremy Clarkson, in which case *boy*, do we need to talk.

CHAPTER TWELVE

THE F-WORD

FUCK.

Just kidding. This chapter's about feminism. But it's such a controversial word, the chances are you might be more comfortable saying 'fuck' than 'feminism'. In fact, you probably even say it more often. Most people do.

We throw around an awful lot of things about what it means to be a feminist. Here are some of the ones you might have heard:

BEING A FEMINIST MEANS

1. You HATE men
2. You are a lesbian
3. You only wear dungarees
4. You have very long armpit and/or leg hair
5. You never wear make-up or high heels
6. You feel a strong compulsive need to burn your bra

7. You are a witch

8. You never want a boyfriend

9. You never want to get married

10. You never want to have children

11. You hate children

12. You hate everyone

13. You are bad-tempered

14. You are shouty

15. You regularly criticize others

16. You are fat/ugly/small-breasted and jealous of women who aren't

17. You don't like other women

18. You want to kill all the men

19. You want women to run the world

20. You're always offended

As all real feminists know, only one of these is true, and the first rule of feminism is that you're not allowed to tell anyone what it is.

Seriously, while many of the things on this list – like being gay, or making particular wardrobe choices and reproductive decisions – are completely compatible with being a feminist, none of them is mandatory. Feminists are a varied bunch.

It's not surprising that a lot of people start to believe this stuff. It's not surprising if you've believed it yourself until now. These ideas are pretty widespread after all. If you type 'feminists' into Google, the very top hit is 'are ugly'. If you type 'feminists are', you get 'ugly', 'sexist', and 'annoying'. Thanks, Google!

But in reality, feminism means one simple thing: believing that everybody should be treated equally regardless of their sex. Or, more formally, it's the belief in the right of women to have social, economic, political, cultural and personal equality with men.

When I talk about this in schools, I often get asked (usually by suspicious boys), 'If it's truly about equality and not about women being better than men, then why not call it equalism, or humanism?' The answer to this is really simple – first of all, humanism is kind of already another thing, guys. And secondly, the 'fem' bit of the word is really important. Yes, we really are campaigning for everybody to be equal, there is no secret evil plan for women to take over the universe. But in order to reach equality, it is women whose rights need to be fought for, because it is women who have traditionally borne the brunt of structural oppression, gender inequality and sexual violence. And that's why the 'fem' bit is there, and why it's important. As previously discussed, this doesn't mean boys can't face sexism too, and feminism fights against the gender stereotypes and social expectations that harm men too.

Once you realize all of this, it becomes clear that saying you're *not* a feminist is a little bit gross and kind of embarrassing. Anyone who actually makes a point of saying that they are *not* a feminist should be treated socially in exactly the same way as someone who proudly comes out and admits that they never wash their hands after going to the toilet:

- General bafflement and disapproval
- Screwing up of noses in their general direction
- When they hand around nuts, NOBODY takes one

Once you know what feminism means, you realize that the only way to not be a feminist is to think that women and men shouldn't be equal, which is . . . pretty sexist. There kind of isn't an in-between. So I think a lot of people who *say* they aren't feminists just don't really get what it means. The Venn diagram looks roughly like this:

VENN DIAGRAM

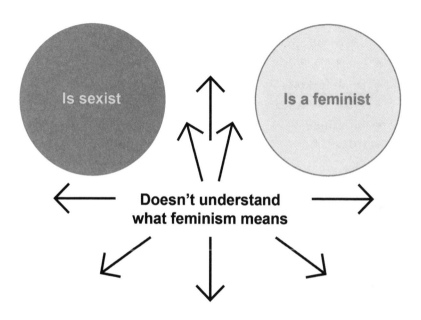

Anybody who says 'I'm not a feminist but . . .' is either a feminist or an arsehole.

Actually, everybody is either a feminist or an arsehole.

And it doesn't mean you have to change your hobbies or your personality or join some kind of cult. Here's a handy checklist of things you can do and still be a feminist:

- Like fashion
- Wear make-up
- Like men
- Have sex
- Really like sex
- Wear dungarees

- Not want to date or marry men
- Not want to date or marry anybody
- Be disabled or non-disabled, religious or non-religious, employed or unemployed
- Laugh
- Drink cocktails
- Wear a headscarf
- Be a student
- Bake
- Masturbate
- Have kids
- Not have kids
- Work
- Be a stay-at-home parent
- Read books
- Fall in love
- Eat bananas
- Have friends (I *promise*)

Here's what you can't do while being a feminist:

- Think men and women shouldn't be equal

It's literally that simple.

In fact . . .

LOOK AT ALL
THESE PEOPLE
BEING FEMINISTS

I realize this is a lot to take in, so to help clarify, follow this simple flow chart to see if YOU might be a feminist:

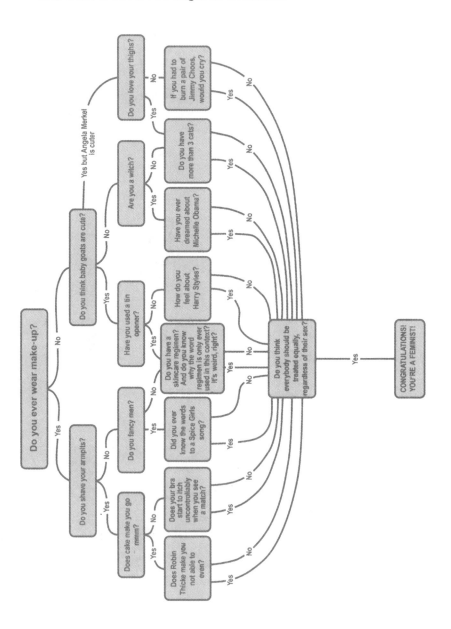

So why are there so many myths about feminism? Partly because it suits the people who benefit most from gender inequality to make feminism seem as unattractive and ridiculous as possible.

Take the often repeated myth that feminists burn their bras, for example.

This never actually happened. Seriously.

The idea comes from a protest that feminists held outside the 1968 Miss America Pageant. They threw a bunch of items like *Playboy* magazines, cosmetics and underwear in a symbolic trash-can outside the event. That's literally it. But a journalist at the time thought it'd be clever to call the women 'bra burners' and so the myth was born.

How do I know these myths have been spread by mostly male, non-feminist writers? Because any female writer would know how much a bra costs. And anyone who knows how much a bra costs would never seriously believe that even one woman would voluntarily burn one, let alone a whole group of women. Good bras are like gold dust. I personally have several that are at least fourteen years old.

While we're on the subject of myths, there are a lot of guys who think feminism has killed manliness, or destroyed chivalry, or ruined flirting and relationships.

Their conversations go something like this:

Dude 1: You can't open a door for a girl any more.
Dude 2: So true.
Dude 1: Chivalry is dead, man, I'm telling you.
Dude 2: So true.
Dude 1: Shit, check out the tits on that thing.
Dude 2: Hey, baby! Come here, foxy mama! *makes kissing noises*

(*Girl ignores them*)

Dude 1: See what I mean?

Dude 2: So true.

Mostly, as previously discussed, these chaps seem to be confused about the difference between flirting and screaming at strangers in the street. But the truth, as someone very wise once pointed out on Twitter, is that if your sexual advances are being 'cock-blocked' by feminism, you're probably doing them wrong.

For interpreting other things people erroneously say about feminism, this table may be of some help.

Shit people say about feminism	What they really mean
Feminists hate men.	I feel like this is an attack on me and that's not fair. Why can't things just stay the way they are? It's working out real well for me.
Feminists are all ugly.	I feel bewildered and weirded out by these strong, independent women so I'll quickly insult them. Haha they'll never see through this one.
Women who shave their legs aren't really feminists.	I like some women who say they are feminists, but I hate feminists, so it must mean these women are not really feminists. We need a new category so I can still enjoy their company. Also I have no time for thinking about why I only like women who shave their legs. Don't press me too much on this, OK?
Feminists are fat.	These women are scaring me so I'll try and force them back into a position of weakness by reasserting the patriarchal structure of judging them based on their looks. Why isn't it working? Why isn't it WORKING?
Feminists are all lesbians.	I can't comprehend the idea that women would critique male dominance unless it was because they didn't want to have sex with me. How could anyone not want to have sex with me?
Feminism is too extreme.	I'm feeling threatened by this. Make it stop. Change is scary!

(Of course, some people have genuine questions about feminism, and it's good to engage with them on a reasonable level, but the ridiculous and outrageous slurs can just go and get in the sea.)

Finally, a few last questions we need to clear up:

1. Is Beyoncé a feminist?

A: Yes, because she says so.

2. Can men be feminists?

A: Yes, if they believe women are (and should be treated as) equal to men.

3. How do I become a feminist?

A: First, you need to live in a house with a chimney. Then wait until you're around ten or eleven and listen out for a weird hooting sound. If an owl comes down the chimney with a letter addressed in green ink, you're in. Pack up your trunk and grab your copy of Mary Warlockstonecraft's *Standard Book of Side-eye, Grade 1*. Go to platform 9¾ at Kings Cross station and catch the school train by squeezing into the impossibly small space between the legs of two manspreaders (men who spread their legs, taking up too much seat space and typically preventing women from sitting down). If you see a chocolate frog on the train, try not to kiss it – it will come to life and give you a lecture about not needing a prince to rescue you because you're a strong, independent feminist. Make sure you get off the train at the right stop. If you reach Blogwarts School of Bitchcraft and Misandry you've gone too far. (It is thankfully a very small school, but few come back from there.) Your first year is mostly pretty standard stuff – simple, common spells like '*ouchio*' (for guys who get too close in crowded spaces), '*alo-no-mora*' (to silence unwanted catcalls) and '*expelhisarmus*', which handily causes gropers' arms to disappear. In your second year you'll learn to turn a sexist pig into an actual pig, in your third you'll learn anti-chauvinism charms, and in your fourth you'll start to play QuidRich, the magical game where feminists score points to bring their salaries in line with their male peers'.

ALTERNATIVELY ... think women and men are equally valuable humans and should be treated as such. Abracadabra, you're a feminist! (You probably already are, even if you didn't know it yet.)

4. If I make a mistake, do I have to stop being a feminist?

A: Luckily for all of us, there are no supreme feminist overlords (overladies?) waiting to boot you out if you slip up. (I hope. I didn't mean it when I said 'guys'. *I didn't mean it, OK?*) We all live in a world where sexism is all around us all the time so it's normal to have taken on some sexist ideas without realizing it. What's great is to try and start challenging those ideas and thinking differently. There's no 'right' or 'wrong' way to be a feminist. It isn't a course, or a religion, or a job, it's a way of thinking and hopefully a way of behaving. Nobody else gets to tell you whether or not you're 'doing it right'.

5. Can I be a feminist and also be [insert religion here]?

A: Yes. You know what being a feminist means by now, so I'm not going to repeat it. As far as I'm concerned, that doesn't stop you believing in God, or being religious. Some of the most powerful and incredible feminists have been religious women. Just look at Sara Hurwitz, the first publicly ordained Orthodox Jewish Rabba; or Tawakkol Karman, the Muslim co-founder of Women Journalists Without Chains and Nobel Peace Prize winner; or Roman Catholic feminist nun Sister

Teresa Forcades, who is campaigning for a more feminist and tolerant church. What about Sister Elizabeth Johnson, a nun who battled to raise the voices of women in the church and dared to question the traditional view of Mary as humble and obedient? Or Huda Sha'arawi, the founder of the Egyptian Feminist Union? Or Kate Kelly, who campaigned tirelessly for women to be ordained to the all-male Mormon priesthood?

It can feel difficult at times to reconcile aspects of feminism with aspects of faith. In some cases the choice to combine the two is unfairly taken out of our hands. There is also huge debate among feminists of faith about all sorts of issues, but many point out that religious texts and traditions have often been shaped by patriarchal and male-dominated societies. One person's interpretation doesn't have to be the same as another's. To believe in God and to have faith doesn't necessarily mean accepting every religious text at face value. Muslim feminist Zainah Anwar, for example, has girled up and dedicated years to challenging traditionally accepted interpretations of the Qur'an.

I think both feminism and religion are big enough and strong enough to stand some serious debate. If these are issues you're interested in exploring further, check out 'Faith in Feminism' – there is info at the back of the book.

6. **Will people still want to go out with me if I'm a feminist?**
A: Yes. I swear! Most of the feminists I know have pretty awesome love lives. I can see why you might worry about this, especially if you're into guys, given all the media crap about man-hating feminists. But turn the question around. If a guy is put off by you being a feminist, you need to ask yourself how put off *you* are by someone who doesn't believe in equality for women.

(AGAIN)

JACKASSES:
0/10

WOULD
NOT
BANG

Take inspiration from the words of the awesome Alyssa Bishop, interviewed in the *New York Times* about taking a stand over her right to decide what happens to her own body:

'If people don't think that my blue armpit hair is funny, then they probably aren't worth my time.'

Damn straight.

※

So you've heard about feminism, you've debunked the myths, now how do you get involved?

To start with, you can make a huge difference just by opening people's eyes to the problem. Basically you're like Alice; you've fallen down the rabbit hole and now it's your turn to go out and be the white rabbit and lead everybody else down behind you. *Go on, you're late, you're late, you're late.*

The next thing that you can do is to speak out when you see sexism, which isn't always easy. It might mean standing up for someone you know, or calling out street harassment, or even challenging your friends.

You can also find out more about feminism by exploring feminist blogs and Tumblrs, or checking out some of the further reading ideas at the back of this book.

There are also loads of incredible women's organizations, campaigns and groups that you can join if you want to get more involved, from attending a UK Feminista Summer School to volunteering for your local branch of the Women's Equality Party. Check out the list at the back!

Another great way to get involved and spread the word is to join a feminist society. If there isn't one in your school or university, why not start your own? In the awesome words of Lily Tomlin: 'I always wondered why somebody didn't do something about that. Then I realized I am somebody.'

This is a good one for a whole variety of different situations. You can use a FemSoc to battle sexism and other forms of inequality, to campaign against unfair issues like biased school dress codes, to raise awareness, and to lobby university administrators for zero tolerance policies on issues like sexual harassment.

TOP TIPS FOR STARTING A FEMINIST SOCIETY

- Design a snazzy logo and get it printed on T-shirts to help you stand out on campus.
- If you hold meetings, remember to have them somewhere wheelchair accessible so everybody can attend.
- You can ask members or attendees to raise and vote on important issues to make sure your society is representing everybody.
- Use social media, or a student newspaper, to spread the word.
- Encourage school or university authorities to engage with you by approaching them with concerns and areas you could work on together.
- Make sure your approach is intersectional.
- Bring cake.

WHAT DOES IT MEAN TO HAVE AN INTERSECTIONAL FEMINIST SOCIETY?

It means tackling gender inequality in a way that takes into account the intersection between this and other forms of prejudice (like racism, homophobia, transphobia, etc). So if you're tackling sexual harassment on campus, take into account the experiences of women of colour, or LGBT* people, who may experience different and more severe forms of harassment than straight, cisgender (not transgender), white women.

Don't just guess – ask people of colour, LGBT* folk and people with disabilities about their needs and experiences and make sure they are represented. Make sure you are involving a diverse group of people in campaigns and decisions – aim for a wide range of representation within committees and the leadership of your society.

In your own language, social media and materials, try not to use words that perpetuate other forms of prejudice, like using 'lame' or 'gay' as negatives.

Team up and work together with other societies that tackle different forms of discrimination so you can combat different forms of prejudice cooperatively.

Try to have a safe space policy to make sure that people are comfortable attending the group – some people might appreciate it if you use trigger warnings before discussing sensitive topics, for example.

Remember it's not the responsibility of people from marginalized groups within your community to educate your group. It won't be a useful, safe space for them if they have to spend all their time explaining what disablism is, how transphobia works, or that there's no such thing as 'reverse racism'. As a group there's a lot of great online resources you can use to learn more about these issues.

SHOULD I INVITE GUYS TO BE PART OF MY FEMSOC?

This is a good question and not an easy one to answer. You might have reasons for thinking that a women-only space would be useful, for example if students might want to discuss experiences of sexual assault and harassment on campus and not feel able to do so with men or boys present. On the other hand, you don't want to only preach to the choir, and getting guys involved can be one of the best ways to spread the message and change behaviour. There are several options here – you could alternate women-only meetings with mixed ones, or, if you have a feminist male friend, you could ask them if they'd be interested in setting up a separate group for guys to look at these issues, and the two groups could meet up for discussions or hold joint events. There's no wrong way of doing it – just work out what feels right for your community.

And be prepared ... while you will hopefully receive lots of interest and support, you may also have a few conversations that go something like this:

You: Hey! We're starting a feminist society, would you be interested in coming along to our—

Guy: Feminism is only for girls.

You: No, actually, people of all genders can—

Guy: I can't come to your club because I don't hate men.

You: Well, actually, feminism doesn't mean—

Guy: We don't need feminism any more because women are already equal.

You: Well, you might be surprised to find that women still suffer high rates of—

Guy: Girls suck, bitches.
You: That :/

It's not all about feminist societies though. You might prefer to start a mentoring club, where older students can help to guide and support younger ones, or a speakers' society, where inspiring women from different fields come in to talk. There are all kinds of different ways to make a difference.

Another thing you might want to do is start a feminist campaign. Remember these two simple things and you'll be well on your way:

1. If it feels like sexist bullshit, it probably is.
2. If you feel passionate about it, somebody else probably will too.

When Lucy-Anne Holmes read a copy of the *Sun* the day after Jessica Ennis had won an Olympic gold medal and realized the biggest picture in the paper of a woman was still one standing in her pants, she felt really sad. Then she felt really angry. Then she went to bed and couldn't sleep and wrote a seventeen-page letter to Rupert Murdoch. Then she probably had some cookies because she was up in the middle of the night, I mean, come on. Then she realized she couldn't stop thinking about it (the Page 3 sexism not the cookie). Then she started a small internet petition just to see if anyone else felt the same way. THEN EVERYONE IN THE WORLD STARTED TALKING ABOUT IT AND 200,000 PEOPLE SIGNED HER PETITION AND IT GREW INTO AN INCREDIBLE NATIONAL CAMPAIGN AND THE *SUN* TOTALLY REMOVED PAGE 3!!!

So don't feel like starting a campaign is a huge daunting thing. It starts with you, and something that really bugs you, and a cookie in the middle of the night, which frankly is essential to the hatching of any good plan. People power will kick in, others will offer their support, the campaign will take on a life of its own and you'll never know until you try. What have you got to lose?

If all this sounds daunting, remember that you're not alone and that some of the most badass, inspiring feminists of today are young women who started from scratch and blazed their own trails. Here are just a few examples to inspire you . . .

Amandla Stenberg was named after the Zulu word for 'power' and basically decided to full-on live up to it. As if being a successful actress from age four and starring in international smash hit *The Hunger Games* wasn't incredible enough, she went on to become a powerful and influential spokesperson for black women and girls, calling out racism and cultural appropriation and generally kicking ass. Oh, did I mention this was all by the age of sixteen?

Faced with tackling the huge issue of female genital mutilation, Muna Hassan did what any sensible young person would – she went on national television and told the Prime Minister to grow a pair. Literally. (Pretty sure she was talking about ovaries BTW). She also told him: 'If you can't handle the issue then there is no point in you doing your job.' Then she and Fahma Mohamed and a group of other incredible young people marched down to Westminster and presented Michael Gove with a petition which totally convinced him to write to every school in the country about FGM. So . . . that was that really.

When she was told girls weren't supposed to go to school after a certain age, Malala Yousafzai was like, 'Yeah, that's not really going to work for me.' At the age of eighteen, she has basically wiped the floor with every other hero the world has ever known, having survived being shot in the head by the Taliban for her stance on education, won the Nobel Peace Prize, started a world-wide campaign for girls' schooling and generally redefined the term badass. Oh, and then she aced her GCSEs. She's pretty much ready to retire now.

These young women are the *definition* of girling up. And you can be too. You're not alone. You're on the right side of history. You can do it!

I went to one school where a group of twelve-year-old girls had noticed that the boys in their year kept 'rating' their body parts out of ten as they came into the classroom – with different scores shouted out for their breasts, bottoms and legs. They were furious, embarrassed and unhappy about it, but instead of taking it lying down, they got together and came up with a plan. A few days later, they all came into school wearing the same T-shirts. On the front, they'd printed a quote inspired by Martin Luther King: 'I want to live in a world where I'm judged by the content of my character, not the parts of my body.'

And on the back? It said: 'I *AM* 10/10'.

GIRL UP

know you still have questions – we all do. Why are we still having to explain consent to people when the whole thing is so damn simple? Why can't Taylor Swift and Katy Perry just kiss and make up? Why am I still reading this book when I only picked it up for its whimsical yet politically charged title?

Just remember:

You don't need to live up to anyone's bullshit beauty standards.

Society should tackle harassers' behaviour, not tell you to modify yours.

Your body belongs to you and you're the only one who gets to decide what happens to it.

The world has stupid ideas about what it means to be a girl and they deserve zero fucks from you.

It's OK to talk about sexism. It's OK to fight back. There's a revolution coming - you won't be alone.

Vagina is not a dirty word.

Masturbation is normal.

Don't masturbate with a frozen carrot.

Nobody has the right to touch you without your consent.

You're not defined by your gender, your body,
or what anybody else says about you. Only you
get to decide who you are.

Reach out for support. There's help to be had.
Things are going to get better.

Remember, you can always change your mind.

Young women are superheroes. You are stronger
than you know.

And when the going gets tough, the tough Girl UP.

ACKNOWLEDGEMENTS

A huge and heartfelt thank you to all the young people who have spoken to me over the past three years, who filled in my worksheets and told me about their experiences. I am in awe of you. Thank you to all the schools, universities and teachers who made me welcome. I am so grateful too to everybody who has shared their stories with the Everyday Sexism Project.

Thank you so much to Abigail Bergstrom, my amazing editor, for being the very definition of what it means to Girl Up, and to Hannah Corbett, Isabel Prodger, Elizabeth Preston, and the whole brilliant team at Simon & Schuster. To Georgia Garrett, for her invaluable wisdom and advice, to the wonderful Emma Paterson, Laurence Laluyaux and everybody at Rogers, Coleridge and White. To Elinor Cooper and everybody at Rochelle Stevens & Co for everything they have done to help and support me.

To Jo Harrison for her beautiful illustrations and for knowing instinctively exactly what I wanted them to say. And to my brilliant copyeditor, Kate Murray-Browne.

To Isabel Chapman, Helen Sharpe, Jo Harrison, Nessie Mason, and Anna James for their expert advice and help on specific issues.

To each of the incredible women (Mary, Shami, Paris, Helen, Ellie, Zena, Anita, Josie, Martha, Bettany, Charlotte, Justine, Samira,

Nimco and Bridget) who gave so generously of their time and expertise for the career chapter.

To Ellie, Juliet, Shyamala, Sarisha, Yas, June, Rose, Eva, Becky, Pauline, Elizabeth, Sofya, Lily, Amy, Hannah, Anna and Natasha for being the strongest, smartest, most inspiring girls I know.

To the inspiring and anonymous young woman who wanted to share her own experience to help the generation coming next.

To Hayley, Lucy, Aileen and Emma for their invaluable brainstorms and for being such kind and thoughtful early readers.

To Charles, Marie and Hugh, for their napkin vagina sketches.

To all the incredible feminists, too numerous to name, who have been a constant source of encouragement and support.

To my family and to Nick, for everything.

And of course to Ed Sheeran, for the CD.

RESOURCES AND FURTHER INFORMATION

HELP AND SUPPORT

Get Connected http://www.getconnected.org.uk/ Helpline: 0808 808 4994
Free confidential support for young people on abuse, bullying, self-harm, drinking, drugs, mental health, work, homelessness, families and care, citizenship and cultural issues, gender and sexual identity, sex, relationships and pregnancy.

Rape Crisis England and Wales http://www.rapecrisis.org.uk
Helpline: 0808 802 9999
Frontline specialized, independent and confidential support services for women and girls of all ages who have experienced any form of sexual violence at any time in their lives.

Survivors UK http://www.survivorsuk.org Helpline: 0845 122 1201
Information, support and counselling for men and boys who have been raped or sexually abused.

Refuge http://refuge.org.uk Helpline: 0808 2000 247
Help for women and children facing domestic violence.

Men's Advice Line http://www.mensadviceline.org.uk Helpline: 0808 801 0327
Advice and support for men experiencing domestic violence and abuse.

Jewish Women's Aid http://www.jwa.org.uk Helpline: 0808 801 0500 Legal, housing and benefits information, befriending and counselling for Jewish women.

Nour Domestic Violence Support http://nour-dv.org.uk
Provides access to Islamic advisors, legal advisors, counselling and support.

Welsh Women's Aid http://www.welshwomensaid.org.uk Helpline: 0808 80 10 800

Scottish Women's Aid http://www.scottishwomensaid.org.uk Helpline: 0800 027 1234

Broken Rainbow http://www.brokenrainbow.org.uk Helpline: 0300 999 5428
National LGBT* domestic violence helpline providing confidential support to all members of the Lesbian, Gay, Bisexual and Trans* (LGBT*) communities, their family and friends, and agencies supporting them.

National Stalking Helpline http://www.stalkinghelpline.org Helpline: 0808 802 0300

This Is Abuse http://thisisabuse.direct.gov.uk
Information and support on relationship abuse for young people.

Brook http://www.brook.org.uk Ask Brook: 0808 8021234
Free and confidential sexual health advice and contraception to young people under twenty-five.

Scarleteen http://www.scarleteen.com
Inclusive, comprehensive and smart sex, sexual health and sexuality information and help for people in their teens and twenties.

Sex, Etc. http://sexetc.org
Sex education by teens, for teens.

Mind http://www.mind.org.uk Helpline: 0300 123 3393
Mental health charity offering advice and support.

Papyrus prevention of young suicide https://www.papyrus-uk.org Helpline: 0800 068 41 41
Help for young people experiencing depression or suicidal thoughts.

Beat http://www.b-eat.co.uk/ Helpline: 0845 634 1414 Youthline: 0845 634 7650
Information and help on all aspects of eating disorders, including anorexia nervosa, bulimia nervosa, binge eating disorder and related eating disorders.

SelfHarm.co.uk http://www.selfharm.co.uk
Support for young people impacted by self-harm.

ChildLine http://www.childline.org.uk Helpline: 0800 1111
Children and young people can contact ChildLine about anything – no problem is too big or too small. Whatever your worry it's better out than in.

Thinkuknow http://www.thinkuknow.co.uk
Advice for young people on sex, relationships, the internet and technology.

The Cybersmile Foundation https://www.cybersmile.org/ Helpline: 0800 783 1113
Cyber bullying support.

Bullying UK http://www.bullying.co.uk/ Helpline: 0808 800 2222
Advice and information on bullying, including at school.

Karma Nirvana http://www.karmanirvana.org.uk Honour network
helpline: 0800 599 9247
Supports all victims of honour-based abuse and forced marriage.

FORWARD http://www.forwarduk.org.uk Helpline: 020 8960 4000
Advice, support and specialist health care for girls and women
affected by FGM.

British Pregnancy Advisory Service http://www.bpas.org
Information and advice: 08457 30 40 30
Help and support on unplanned pregnancies and abortion.

Galop http://www.galop.org.uk Helpline: 020 7704 2040
Advice and support for people who have experienced biphobia,
homophobia, transphobia, sexual violence or domestic abuse.
They also support lesbian, gay, bi, trans and queer people who
have had problems with the police or have questions about the
criminal justice system.

Mermaids UK http://www.mermaidsuk.org.uk
Help and support for teenagers and children with gender identity
issues.

Being Gay Is Okay http://www.bgiok.org.uk
Information and advice for gay, lesbian, bisexual and unsure under
twenty-fives.

Family and Friends of Lesbians and Gays http://www.fflag.org.uk

FEMINISM AND ACTIVISM

UK Feminista http://ukfeminista.org.uk

Southall Black Sisters http://www.southallblacksisters.org.uk
Helpline: 0208 571 0800

Faith in Feminism www.faithinfeminism.com

Twitter Youth Feminist Army http://tyfa.co.uk

Intersectionality 101 www.nusconnect.org.uk/resources/
intersectionality-101

The Women's Equality Party https://womensequality.org.uk

The F-Word www.thefword.org.uk

Campaign for Consent on the Curriculum www.campaign4consent.
co.uk

Powered By Girl http://poweredbygirl.org

Stop Street Harassment www.stopstreetharassment.org

Shape Your Culture http://www.shapeyourculture.org.uk

Any-body http://www.any-body.org

Rookie www.rookiemag.com

HeForShe http://www.heforshe.org

Hollaback! http://www.ihollaback.org

Stonewall www.stonewall.org.uk

Show Racism the Red Card http://www.theredcard.org

The Everyday Sexism Project www.everydaysexism.com

Sisters Uncut http://facebook.com/sistersuncut

OTHER USEFUL ORGANIZATIONS

Girls Who Code http://girlswhocode.com

Girl Develop It https://www.girldevelopit.com

Black Girls Code http://www.blackgirlscode.com

Stemettes http://www.stemettes.org

ScienceGrrl http://sciencegrrl.co.uk

Grrrl Zine Network http://grrrlzines.net

Smart Girls http://amysmartgirls.com

This Girl Can http://www.thisgirlcan.co.uk

The Representation Project http://therepresentationproject.org

Vidcode http://www.vidcode.io

NOTES

CHAPTER ONE – FAKEBOOK, FITTER AND INSTAGLAM

1   Men have 15 per cent more followers than women on average, and the average male tweeter is almost twice as likely to follow another man than a woman, according to 'New Twitter Research: Men Follow Men and Nobody Tweets', a 2009 study of over 300,000 users by Bill Heil and Mikolaj Piskorski, published in the *Harvard Business Review*, 01/06/2009 (https://hbr.org/2009/06/new-twitter-research-men-follo)

2   Analysis by the tool Twee-Q ('Twitter Equality Quotient') of almost half a million retweets found that men are retweeted almost twice as often as women, according to an *Adweek* article, 'On Twitter, Men Are Retweeted Far More Than Women (And You're Probably Sexist, Too)' by Shea Bennett, 31/07/12 (http://www.adweek.com/socialtimes/twee-q-sexist-twitter/467654)

3   For example, 'IT HAPPENED TO ME: I Posed As a Man on Twitter and Nobody Called Me Fat or Threatened to Rape Me for Once' by Alex Blank Millard, on xojane.com, 25/03/15 (http://www.xojane.com/it-happened-to-me/i-was-a-man-on-twitter) and 'How my spoof BBC Question Time Twitter account showed me the level of abuse political women face on social media' by Martin Belam, 04/07/15 (http://martinbelam.com/2013/bbcextraghost/)

CHAPTER TWO – YOU AREN'T YOUR BODY

1   '"Average" Briton Highlighted on UN World Statistics Day', Office for National Statistics, 20/10/2010 (http://www.ons.gov.uk/ons/about-ons/get-involved/events/events/un-world-statictics-day/-average--briton-highlighted-on-un-world-statistics-day.pdf)

2   According to a PR Newswire article, 'Pressure to look perfect drives girls to Destructive Behavior', 02/10/07, which references a September 2007 study by the Nielsen Company (http://www.prnewswire.com/news-releases/pressure-to-look-perfect-drives-girls-to-destructive-behavior-58309862.html)

3 'Reflections on Body Image', report from the All Party Parliamentary Group on Body Image, May 2012 (http://issuu.com/bodyimage/docs/reflections_on_ body_image?e=5210515/2698118)
4 Ibid.
5 'Children, Teens, Media, and Body Image', research report by Common Sense Media, 21/01/15 (https://www.commonsensemedia.org/research/children-teens-media-and-body-image)
6 'Changing the Game for Girls', Women's Sport and Fitness Foundation, April 2015 (https://www.womeninsport.org/wp-content/uploads/2015/04/ Changing-the-Game-for-Girls-Policy-Report.pdf)

CHAPTER THREE – MAKING WAVES

1 'Lad Culture Audit Report', National Union of Students, 27/07/15 (http://www. nus.org.uk/en/news/nus-announces-the-next-phase-of-its-fight-against-lad-culture/)

CHAPTER SEVEN – SLUTS, UNICORNS AND OTHER MYTHICAL CREATURES

1 'Crime in England and Wales 2009/10: Findings from the British Crime Survey and Police Recorded Crime', eds. John Flatley, Chris Kershaw, Kevin Smith, Rupert Chaplin and Debbie Moon, Statistics Bulletin, Home Office & the Office for National Statistics, July 2010 (http://www.gov.uk/government/uploads/ system/uploads/attachment_data/file/116347/hosb1210.pdf)
2 'Intimate Partner Violence in the United States: Nonfatal Intimate Partner Violence has Declined Since 1993' by Shannan Catalano, PhD, Bureau of Justice Statistics, US Department of Justice, December 2006.
3 'Physical Dating Violence Among High School Students – United States, 2003', Centers for Disease Control and Prevention, Morbidity and Mortality Weekly Report, May 19, 2006, Vol. 55, No. 19, pp.532–5.

CHAPTER EIGHT – IT'S MY FACE AND I'LL SMILE IF I WANT TO

1 'Fewer Women Leading FTSE 100 Firms than Men Called John' by Jennifer Rankin, Guardian, 06/03/15 (http://www.theguardian.com/business/2015/mar/06/ johns-davids-and-ians-outnumber-female-chief-executives-in-ftse-100)
2 'Seen But Not Heard: How Women Make Front Page News', Women in Journalism, 15/10/12 (http://womeninjournalism.co.uk/wp-content/uploads/2012/10/ Seen_but_not_heard.pdf)

3 'Stemming the Tide' by Laura Howes, Royal Society of Chemistry, 21/08/13 (http://www.rsc.org/chemistryworld/2013/08/gender-diversity-women-science)
4 'An Overview of Sexual Offending in England and Wales', Statistics Bulletin, Home Office & the Office for National Statistics, Ministry of Justice, January 2013 (https://www.gov.uk/government/uploads/system/uploads/attachment_data/file/214970/sexual-offending-overview-jan-2013.pdf)
5 'Girls Choosing Camera Lenses over Microscopes', Mark Gould, the *Guardian*, 03/10/08, quoting a survey carried out by New Outlooks in Science and Engineering (Noise) (http://www.theguardian.com/education/2008/oct/03/science.choosingadegree)
6 'Sexual Harassment in the Capital', YouGov survey for the End Violence Against Women Coalition, 25/05/12 (https://yougov.co.uk/news/2012/05/25/sexual-harassment-capital/)
7 '2010 Poll on Sexual Harassment in Schools', YouGov survey for the End Violence Against Women Coalition, 15/10/10 (http://www.endviolenceagainstwomen.org.uk/2010-poll-on-sexual-harassment-in-schools)
8 Ibid.
9 'More than 300 Rapes Reported in Schools in Past Three Years', the *Independent*, 25/08/14 (http://www.independent.co.uk/news/uk/crime/more-than-300-rapes-reported-in-schools-in-past-three-years-9686793.html)

CHAPTER NINE – CLITORISH ALLSORTS

1 'The Most Important Sexual Statistic', Michael Castleman, *Psychology Today*, 16/03/09, quoting a comprehensive analysis of over thirty-three studies in the book *The Case of the Female Orgasm* by Elisabeth Lloyd (Harvard University Press, 2006).

CHAPTER TEN – CIRCLE OF SHAME

1 'Gender Inequality in 500 Popular Films: Examining On-Screen Portrayals and Behind-the-Scenes Employment Patterns in Motion Pictures Released between 2007–2012' by Dr Stacy L. Smith, Marc Choueiti, Elizabeth Scofield & Dr Katherine Pieper, Annenberg School for Communication & Journalism, University of Southern California, 2013 (http://annenberg.usc.edu/pages/~/media/MDSCI/Gender_Inequality_in_500_Popular_Films_-_Smith_2013.ashx)
2 'The Celluloid Ceiling: Behind-the-Scenes Employment of Women on the Top 250 Films of 2014' by Martha M. Lauzen, PhD, Center for the Study of Women in Television and Film, San Diego State University, 2015 (http://womenintvfilm.sdsu.edu/files/2014_Celluloid_Ceiling_Report.pdf)
3 The Representation Project, 2012 (http://therepresentationproject.org/wp-content/uploads/repinfo31.jpg)

Praise for Laura Bates

'If Caitlin Moran's *How To Be A Woman* is the
fun-filled manual for female survival in the 21st century,
Everyday Sexism is its more politicised sister'
Independent on Sunday

'It is a wonderful book . . . a thrilling, intelligent, accessible,
uplifting and empowering look at our current situation and the
evidence it offers of the potential for change. Read the book'
Lucy Mangan

'Following [*Everyday Sexism*] will make most
women feel oddly saner'
Caitlin Moran

'The shocking posts in this book provide powerful
evidence that sexism is on the increase in society . . .
This is a passionate tome'
Sunday Times

'A pioneering analysis of modern-day misogyny'
Telegraph

'This is an important work and if I had my way would be compulsory school reading across the globe'

Feminist Times

'Her game-changing book *Everyday Sexism* is a must-read for every woman'

Cosmopolitan

'This is an important book not only for the victims of sexism but for parents, siblings, partners and friends, allowing them to understand what today's women are up against. The message is crucial: those who have been discriminated against, shamed and assaulted are not alone, and there is power in shouting back'

Independent

'Laura was one of the first women to harness the power of social media to fight sexism and misogyny and give millions of young women a voice'

Grazia

'Extremely powerful, the kind of book that could, and should, win hearts and minds right across the spectrum'

Financial Times

Read Laura Bates' first book

which was shortlisted for
Waterstones Book of the Year and
Polemic of the Year at the Political Book Awards

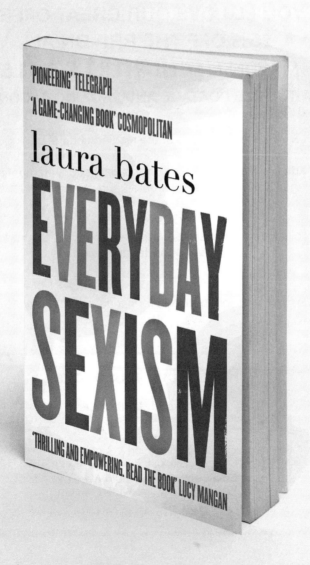

'PIONEERING' TELEGRAPH

'A GAME-CHANGING BOOK' COSMOPOLITAN

laura bates

EVERYDAY
SEXISM

'THRILLING AND EMPOWERING. READ THE BOOK' LUCY MANGAN

**SIMON &
SCHUSTER**

IF YOU ENJOY GOOD BOOKS, YOU'LL LOVE OUR GREAT OFFER 25% OFF THE RRP ON ALL SIMON & SCHUSTER UK TITLES
WITH FREE POSTAGE AND PACKING (UK ONLY)

Simon & Schuster UK is one of the leading general book publishing companies in the UK, publishing a wide and eclectic mix of authors ranging across commercial fiction, literary fiction, general non-fiction, illustrated and children's books.

For exclusive author interviews, features and competitions log onto:
www.simonandschuster.co.uk

*Titles also available in **eBook** format across all digital devices.*

How to buy your books

Credit and debit cards
Telephone Simon & Schuster Cash Sales at **Sparkle Direct** on **01326 569444**

Cheque
Send a cheque payable to *Simon & Schuster Bookshop* to:
Simon & Schuster Bookshop, PO Box 60, Helston, TR13 OTP

Email: sales@sparkledirect.co.uk
Website: www.sparkledirect.com

Prices and availability are subject to change without notice.